Fruitful in Affliction

"For God has made me
to be fruitful in the land
of my affliction."
Genesis 41:52

Miray A. Jaksa

DEDICATION

I would like to dedicate this book
to every mom who has a special needs child.

The Lord knows your sorrows as well as your
joys. I pray that the Lord will cause you to be *fruitful
in affliction*. Our children are a gift from the Lord.

He who loves the little children has thoughts
toward them that are filled with peace
to give them a future and a hope.

Jeremiah 29:11

CONTENTS

Acknowledgments   ix

Introduction   xiii

1   A Fruitful Vine   1
    Genesis 49:22

2   In the Land of My Affliction   6
    Genesis 41:52

3   God Meant It for Good   10
    Genesis 50:20

4   Free Indeed   15
    John 8:36

5   Through Many Hardships   20
    Acts 14:22

6   The Gift of Grace   25
    Galatians 3:6

7   The Helper   30
    John 16:7

8   Bring Forth Much Fruit   35
    John 12:24

9   Filled with the Spirit   40
    Ephesians 5:18

10 Living by the Spirit   46
    Romans 8:5-6

11 Fragrance of Christ   51
    2 Corinthians 2:15

12 Love Suffers Long   56
    1 Corinthians 13:4

13 Love Is Kind   63
    Titus 3:4-5

14	Love Is Not Rude *1 Corinthians 13:4-5*	69
15	Love Is Not Self-Seeking *1 Corinthians 13:5*	75
16	Love Is Not Easily Angered *1 Corinthians 13:5*	78
17	Love Keeps No Record of Wrongs *1 Corinthians 13:5*	82
18	Pure Joy *James 1:2-3*	86
19	To God, My Joy and My Delight *Psalm 43:4*	91
20	Intro to Reasons to Rejoice *Nehemiah 8:10*	96
21	Reasons to Rejoice, Part 1: Refuge *Psalm 71:1*	99
22	Reasons to Rejoice, Part 2: Rescue *Psalm 71:2*	102
23	Reasons to Rejoice, Part 3: Rock *Psalm 71:3*	105
24	Reasons to Rejoice, Part 4: Reliable *Psalm 71:6*	108
25	Reasons to Rejoice, Part 5: Righteousness *Psalm 71:19*	111
26	Reasons to Rejoice, Part 6: Restore *Psalm 71:20*	114
27	Reasons to Rejoice, Part 7: Revive *Psalm 71:20*	117
28	Reasons to Rejoice, Part 8: Redeemed *Psalm 71:23*	122
29	The Greatest of All Reasons to Rejoice *Luke 2:8-11*	126

CONTENTS

30 In Me You May Have Peace   132
    John 16:33

31 The Peace of God   136
    Psalm 29:11

32 For He Himself Is Our Peace   141
    Isaiah 26:3

33 Perfect Peace, the Perfect Gift   146
    Philippians 4:6-7

34 The Merciful Patience of God   151
    2 Peter 3:9

35 Patience Rewarded   158
    Hebrews 10:35-36

36 Yet Will I Hope in Him   163
    Job 13:15

37 With Patience Comes Hope   167
    Psalm 119:49

38 Patiently Persevering, Part 1   170
    Job 23:10

39 Patiently Persevering, Part 2   173
    Job 23:10

40 Patiently Persevering, Part 3   176
    Job 23:10

41 The Kindness of the King   182
    2 Samuel 9:13

42 Appropriating His Promises   187
    Titus 3:4

43 The ABCs of God's Goodness   193
    Galatians 5:22

44 The Lord is Faithful   196
    Isaiah 41:10

45 As I Was with Moses   202
    Joshua 1:5

46 Genuine Gentleness   206
   Matthew 11:29

47 The Gentleness of Christ   209
   Luke 22:42

48 The Heart of Gentleness   212
   John 3:30

49 Enough Is Enough   217
   1 Corinthians 6:12

50 Purpose with a Passion   220
   Daniel 1:8

51 Unless a Grain of Wheat Falls   225
   John 12:24

52 That Your Fruit Would Remain   229
   John 15:16

ACKNOWLEDGMENTS

I first have to thank my commander-in-chief, my Lord Jesus, for without Him this book would never have been written. Jesus is the author and finisher of my faith as well as this book—to Him be all the glory. As He started pouring out, I honestly couldn't write fast enough and quickly ran out of my sons' school paper. I asked the Lord to send me paper if He really wanted me to keep writing, because I wanted to make sure this was from Him. A few days later two boxes showed up on my doorstep containing 2,000 sheets of paper. And it wasn't just lined school paper but really nice stationery. I asked the Lord, "What is this?" and He said, "You asked for paper and I'm giving you paper." From that time on, the Lord continued to give me encouragement every step of the way through several friends that I must acknowledge.

I must thank my dear neighbor and friend, Connie Hiss, for being obedient to the Lord when He told her to send paper my way not knowing He had a greater plan for it. The Lord has used you once again to bless me. You are such a joy and I thank the Lord for you.

Thank you to my precious friend and sister in the Lord, Nancy Tumbas, for her countless hours of editing this book. Thank you for your help and encouragement, I couldn't have done all this without you. You are such a blessing to me. With God all things are possible!

I would also like to thank my pastor, Terry

Walker. The Lord used you so many Wednesday nights and Sunday mornings to speak to me and confirm what the Spirit was impressing on my heart. And thank you, Sheila, for your support, prayers and encouragement always. You are such a blessing and the best pastor's wife!

Thank you, John Ohanian, for your *Word for the Day* encouragements on Sunday mornings as you give announcements. The Lord speaks through you continually to encourage me as well as the body of Christ at Calvary Chapel Living Word.

Thank you, Kellie O'Reilly, for all you did to edit this book and help get it ready for publishing. You were a godsend. I so appreciate the gifts God has given you. Your eye for detail and willingness to sit for hours at the computer greatly eased this process.

Thank you to my friend and *C.R.I.M.S.O.N.* author, R.H. Krebs, for all your advice and help with this book. Your practical insights and experience have blessed me tremendously.

Thank you, Mike and Susie Gillmore, for all your help and work on the book cover. It turned out amazing. You were such an answer to prayer.

Thank you, Meg, for being a Galatians 6:2 friend— that day was the beginning of God's healing process and a new chapter in my life. I so appreciate you being there when I needed a shoulder to cry on. John, you said, "If you'll just sit with the Lord, He has so much He wants to give to us: 3 meals a day and snacks too!" I took that to heart and committed to sit and listen to the Lord, and this is what Jesus gave me—the mega portion! You were right.

ACKNOWLEDGMENTS

This book was written and inspired during my personal gleanings and quiet time, when all I could do is sit before the Lord. It was during this time I worked through Beth Moore's *Living Beyond Yourself: Exploring the Fruit of the Spirit* study. The Lord used this study immensely to heal my heart from a gaping wound that needed to be mended. I asked the Lord to make me *fruitful in affliction* and to help me to live beyond myself. I believe He answered that prayer. Thank you, Beth, for your love for the Word and our Lord Jesus, your prayers and letter. The Lord has greatly used you to encourage me and bring me to a place where I'm truly living beyond myself!

I am so very grateful for the friends and ladies at Calvary Chapel Living Word who I've been blessed to be with in a small group during our Bible study. Your prayers have fueled this book. (And you didn't even know when I asked for prayer that I'd be "fruitful in affliction" this was what I had in mind.) Let me just say God answers prayer!

All definitions used are from Noah Webster's 1828 *American Dictionary of the English Language.* All synonym references are from *Roget's Pocket Thesaurus*, 1946 edition.

Scripture references are taken from the following: King James Version, New King James Version, New International Version, New American Standard and Amplified Bible.

Last—but certainly not least—I would like to thank my husband Emil for his love and devotion to our Lord and for the prayers while I was working on this project. Thank you AJ and Noah for your patience while I spent hours on the computer writing this book.

I've always believed in Romans 8:28, that God does work all things together for good, even my daughter's challenge with her speech and special needs. This is living proof that the trials we go through can be used to encourage others! Grace Ann, you are such a joy and I love you so very much. I know the Lord has His hand upon your life and has a plan for you. "He who has begun a good work in you will be faithful to complete it." Thank you for being such a blessing and for reminding me what really matters!

INTRODUCTION

I remember the day like it was yesterday. My worst fears were right before me. It was as if we were starting all over again after years of moving forward. All I could think of was years of progress gone down the drain. That morning in church the tears ran silently down my face, matching the silent sorrow I'd been carrying with me for what seemed like an eternity. Not this—please, Lord—she's come so far. Would she ever be *normal*? Would she ever outgrow this? It's every mother's dream to have a beautiful little girl who grows up, goes to college, gets married and has kids of her own. It was my dream, too. My husband and I already had two healthy children, but this time it was different. Only God knew what lay in store for my daughter Grace Ann.

That morning in church, I felt like my world was crashing down around me. I still remember sitting in my friend's office at church, explaining to her why Grace Ann, who was nine at the time, was in the two & three-year-old class. It was extremely hard for me to verbalize but, with tears in my eyes, I told Meg that Grace Ann had been having some tics over the summer—odd little things she was doing, but they seemed to have grown worse overnight. I had noticed these tics over the years and wasn't sure what they were. A Christian friend of mine who has a degree in child psychology assured me that children have nervous tics as a coping mechanism when they are out of their element. The times they were the worst was when we were out of the country visiting my husband's family. I didn't worry too much about the tics prior to this, but now they were happening all the time.

I was scared that this was going to be the new norm for my daughter who had already overcome so much. She was hospitalized at nine weeks old with a major respiratory infection. When she was fifteen months old I knew something wasn't right with her. She had a few words, but she wasn't gaining new ones. She was chronically sick that first year of her life with RSV (respiratory system virus), bronchitis and asthma. Every month that winter she went to the hospital for special shots to help her with the RSV. When she was eighteen months old, I asked the doctor again about her speech and he told me not to worry. By two years old, Grace Ann was in speech therapy. I remember one day being at McDonald's with a friend of mine when our girls were two-and-a-half. They were just a few months apart, but Sarah spoke in paragraphs and Grace Ann was silent. I kept wondering, "When is Grace Ann going to talk like my friend's kids?" It wasn't until she was almost three that we discovered she had a severe ear infection. Basically her ear drum was retracted so badly, it was as if she had Elmer's glue in her ear. Even though the doctor had looked in her ears and said they were clear of fluids, there was still fluid behind her ear drum. Who knows how long her ears would have been like that if I hadn't asked for the tympanogram test to be done? It was such a simple test. The doctor took us into the very next room and inserted an ear-bud into her ear to test the sound going into her ear drum. Like the ticker tape read out for contraction pains, mountain peaks were good, meaning sound was getting to her ears. A flat line was bad. After doing the test six or seven times, her left ear was a completely flat line. A few months later, she ended up having tubes put in because her ears kept filling up with fluid on their own. My friends had told me their kids started speaking right away after having tubes put in, but this wasn't the case with Grace Ann. We took her for an assessment with a Christian neurodevelopmentalist who told us that although Grace Ann was three years old chronologically, developmentally she was the age of a one-year-old. The news was devastating. She had missed a significant amount of development during the time her ears were infected. I couldn't believe this was happening to my little girl.

We started therapy right away at home and the following spring we enrolled Grace Ann in a special education class at our local public school. As a homeschool mom of two older boys I struggled with sending her to public school. It was a heart-wrenching decision, but I knew she needed all the help she could get. As the school psychologist assessed Grace Ann, it pained me to face the reality before me. Questions were being raised that I had never thought I'd have to face as a mother. Is my child autistic? How could this be? I had already dealt with my mom dying of cancer eleven years previous. My father-in-law had passed away from cancer too, just two years earlier. Not another tragedy. We took Grace Ann to a pediatric neurologist who diagnosed her with an auditory processing disorder. She continued in her special education at school and I continued with her therapy at home. The progress was painfully slow; she couldn't even say a two-syllable word when she was four years old. She was virtually silent. The process was excruciating. I kept expecting this overnight miracle to take place, but it never did. The miracle would have to wait. In the meantime, the school speech pathologist talked to me about Grace Ann and told me something new about her diagnosis. She had developmental verbal apraxia. Basically her mouth did not know how to make the sounds for speech. She explained that most everyone gets this ability for *free* when they learn to speak. Grace Ann did not get it for free. She would have to learn how to make every sound and work hard for years to come.

In all the challenges, heartaches and trials I have gone through with Grace Ann, I am in awe of God's hand moving behind the scenes. He has been ever so faithful to us. Even when the news was at its worst, the Lord still gave me peace. The miracle was in the making. When I asked for prayer at church for Grace Ann, the elders were there with my pastor and they wondered why Grace Ann needed prayer for healing. Only a few friends at church knew that she didn't talk. For the most part, she was so joyful, smiling all the time, you would have never known there was a problem with her. We asked for prayer for her speech and healing upon her life. I know the Lord answered those prayers that day. The answer just came in God's timing, not mine.

In the last year, Grace Ann's tics have greatly

improved as well as her speech. She's now ten and praying out loud, conversing and reading, too. Her speech isn't perfect, but she's on her way and making progress by God's grace. The silent sorrow I carried in my heart for years grew into an awareness of other moms with special needs children. I knew the Lord was doing something in my heart during this most painful time, so I began to write. I never set out to write a book. But as I spent time in God's Word, He so spoke to me and ministered to me that I couldn't write fast enough. That was when I thought all this writing might be turning into something to encourage someone else. Only the Lord can bring beauty from ashes and purpose from the pain we suffer. I've learned over the years, from one trial to the next (and believe me there have been many), that the Lord never wastes anything. When things looked the darkest with Grace Ann my prayer became, "Lord, I just want to be fruitful in affliction." Joseph has been my long-time hero of the faith. The Lord brought him through trial after trial and, in the end, He had a good purpose for it all. I've always believed the Lord had a plan for Grace Ann, He was just working on her testimony. Mine, too. This book is part of that testimony. God is faithful. One of my life verses is, "I know in whom I have believed and am persuaded that He is able to keep what I have committed to Him until that day" (2 Tim. 1:12).

I don't know what you are facing today, but the Lord does. I am not a professional writer. If it wasn't for the giftedness of my dear friends who edited this book, it would never have come out with so few mistakes. I'm a mom who has a heart to serve the Lord where He has me: at home first and wherever else He leads. I pray that where I lack the Holy Spirit will take over and speak encouragement to your heart. This book is written to you as I would write a letter or a devotional. And the chapters build on each other, so it's best to start at the beginning and read it all the way through. Galatians 5:22 says, "But the fruit of the Spirit is love joy, peace, patience, kindness, goodness, faithfulness, gentleness and self-control." This book is a journey through the fruit of the Spirit from the perspective of one who has had her share of pain, both emotional and physical. I hope to pass on some of the life lessons I've learned along the way, as well as examples from Scripture which ministered to me in my journey to be fruitful. Let me just say, I am still a work in progress.

It's in the personal afflictions we face that the Lord gets our undivided attention. Eight years ago I was diagnosed with fibromyalgia. Although this is a painful condition on many levels, I still desire to be effective and useful for the Lord. In my weakness, I've had to rely on the Lord's strength and grace to be my sufficiency—day by day, moment by moment. I've been blessed to go on two missions trips with my husband, kids and a team from my church, Calvary Chapel Living Word. One of the sweetest blessings was seeing the Lord use Grace Ann at a Vacation Bible School. On our first night she took the hand of each child and walked them down the hallway as their personal escort to our meeting room. She didn't even need words! Her love in action spoke across the language barrier. The Lord is so good!

My publishing company At Home Ministries is in partnership with Hope Outreach Ministry, a special ministry established to reach out to moms of special needs children—to encourage, love, and support them with God's Word, prayer and the fellowship of other moms with special needs children. Both ministries are part of the miracle the Lord had in mind many years ago but is only now coming to fruition. It's my heart's desire to encourage women and remind them that in the hard times and difficult places the Lord still longs to make us fruitful in affliction and bring good out of every trial. It's with this heart that I pray the Lord is glorified through this book and that you the reader are blessed. By His amazing grace and for His glory!

A Fruitful Vine

Joseph is a fruitful vine,
a fruitful vine near a spring,
whose branches climb over a wall.
Genesis 49:22

Chapter 1

If we look around our world today, it doesn't take too long to notice the troubles and trials people are facing. Economically, financially, physically, emotionally, spiritually, hardships come in various shapes and sizes. Perhaps you're facing economic hard times, your husband has lost his job, you don't know how you're going to pay the bills or whether or not you'll be able to keep your home. And then fear sets in and all the *what if's* that the enemy brings. We can hardly forget that on top of it all there is an enemy of our soul who seeks to bring us down. He goes about like a roaring lion seeking whom he may devour. But we have Jesus on our side—our faithful, wonderful, gracious, merciful, precious Savior to see us through the hardships of life and bring us safely to heaven. Each one of us faces different obstacles and trials. Maybe it's not a financial difficulty but a physical illness that you're suffering with. Each day you struggle with the pain and wonder if it is ever going to get better? And if the doctor says the C word, it can be a very fearful thing to face. When my mom was diagnosed with cancer, I remember being really scared at just the thought of it.

I recently watched an award ceremony where various athletes were being acknowledged for overcoming hardships in their life. One woman was a professional tennis player who had won numerous tournaments (so far so good), but she played in a wheelchair. Another young man who was successful overcame the death of his dad to cancer. And lastly there was a woman who had defected from her Communist country seeking the freedom America offers. She too had overcome the trials of her citizenship and leaving her country. Who did she credit for her success? Her sport and herself: the "believe in yourself" speech. All this to point out that everyone faces tough situations. Jesus said, "These things I have spoken to you, that in Me you may have peace. In the world you will have tribulation, but be of good cheer. I have overcome the world" (John 16:33).

The good news is, as Christians, when we go through trials we have Jesus with us. First, we have His presence: "And lo, I am with you always" (Matt. 28:20). Second, we have His promise: "And I will pray the Father, and He will give you another Helper, that He may abide with you forever" (John 14:16). Third, we have His peace: "And the peace of God, which surpasses all understanding, will guard your hearts and your minds in Christ Jesus" (Phil. 4:7). Fourth, we have His power: "But you will receive power when the Holy Spirit has come upon you"

(Acts 1:8). And lastly we have His purpose: "Christ in you, the hope of glory" (Col. 1:27).

If God's goal and will for our lives is to conform us to the image of His Son (Rom. 8:29), we have to trust that if we're abiding in Him and loving Him with all our heart, soul, mind and strength, whatever comes our way will be for our good. We have Romans 8:28 to fall back on: "We are assured and know that all things work together and are fitting into a plan for good to and for those who love God and are called according to His design and purpose." God will use it all to conform the image and person of His Son in our lives. So when the trials come (and they will come, let me assure you), "You will enter the kingdom of heaven through much tribulation." We too can overcome by the blood of the Lamb and the word of His promise.

Now that we've laid a foundation for where we are, we come to the big questions: How do I become fruitful in my affliction? How do I overcome the hardships? How do I find peace in all the pain? Let me say it's only by the grace of God and all that He affords me through His Word which is enlightened to us by His Holy Spirit. Some things are purely out of our control. God is on the throne and "all things have been created through Him and for Him; and He is before all things, and in Him all things consist" (Col. 1:16-17). You and I fit in there, too. He, as Creator, made the universe (when you break it down, "*uni*" means one and "*verse*" means sentence). God spoke a single sentence like, "Let there be light." Four simple words and light came. He kept on speaking and the

3

world was created. When God speaks a word, He creates. It may be a word to a broken and fearful heart: "Fear not. . . . Do not fear . . . I will help you" (Isaiah 41:13-14). He creates comfort, peace, hope and security every time I open His Word and take the time to listen.

Back to our primary question: how do I become fruitful in my affliction? We let the Holy Spirit work in us, filling us day by day with His love, joy, peace, patience, kindness, goodness, gentleness and self-control. How does a peach become a peach? It just hangs in there; it abides in the branch which is connected to the tree and root system. I have a confession to make: I do not have a green thumb. I've killed almost every plant I've bought. My husband, on the other hand, has the gift of greenness (if there is such a gift). I did buy a plant years ago to decorate my front door entry on the porch, something tall and leafy and full of flowers. When my husband saw it, he was already planning its funeral. But miraculously it's lived these past seven or eight years. It's had a few resurrection experiences and near death misses, but it's really very simple—the plant loves the sunlight. She just sits in her white lattice planter box and basks in the morning light each and every day. She never leaves her spot. She never thinks the grass is greener over at the neighbors. The second thing is she loves water. When she is faithfully watered, she blossoms and produces the most beautiful little purple flowers and her branches are full and she just flourishes. Sunlight and water are all she needs to bear a fruitful flower. We too will flourish and God can make us fruitful in our affliction if we choose to "love the Son." It's so simple: love Jesus. Yes, life may be hard. Yes, there may be real hardships and fears. But in it, love the Son, and He will show Himself faithful. The second thing we need is to have a steady, balanced diet of His Word. "Let the word of Christ dwell in you richly in all wisdom; teaching and admonishing one another in psalms and hymns and spiritual songs" (Col. 3:16). Take a daily drink from the fountain of living waters. His Word is the ultimate thirst quencher. It's His word spoken to our hearts and souls that makes us whole. In Isaiah 58:11, God promises to make us a "well-watered garden," but we need to come to Him to be refreshed.

Practically, we can pray each day, "Lord, make me fruitful in this affliction I'm in." He knows and sees and cares about all that concerns you. Pour out your heart in pure and total honesty to Him. Allow Him to fill you and bring about His fruitfulness in your life. He will pour into you His love and flood your heart with His peace. Just ask, seek and knock. Love the Son, stay and abide in the light of His Word and you will find refreshment like no other. That reminds me, I better go water my plant.

In the Land of My Affliction

*For God has caused me to be
fruitful in the land of my affliction.
Genesis 41:52*

Chapter 2

If you haven't read the story of Joseph in the book of Genesis, I highly recommend it. Get familiar with Joseph and all he went through (Gen. 37-50). This chapter offers a brief synopsis of his life.

Joseph was the son of Jacob and Rebekah. He was seventeen years old (in our day, a senior in high school ready to begin his adult life) when his ten older half-brothers sought to get rid of him. You see, they hated Joseph and were jealous of him. They ended up selling him to Midianite merchants for twenty shekels of silver—this was after he'd been rejected by his brothers and thrown in a pit, left for dead. If that wasn't bad enough, they stripped him of his coat that his father had given to him. Genesis 37:23 describes it as "the richly ornamented robe he was wearing." Let's pause here.

So much of Joseph's life becomes a type of our Lord Jesus. Let's take notice of just a few similarities. Joseph was hated and rejected by his brothers and so was Jesus. "When his brothers saw that their father loved him more than any of them, they hated him and could not speak a kind word to him" (Gen. 37:4). "But this is to fulfill what is written in their Law: 'They hated me without reason'" (John 15:25). Joseph was thrown in a pit. Jesus most likely spent his final night in some sort of dungeon or pit awaiting his trial. Joseph was stripped of his robe that was given to him by his father. In John 13, Jesus lays aside his robe to wash the disciples' feet. And at the scourging, He was stripped and humiliated at the cross. His robe was taken by the soldiers and gambled for.

Joseph eventually made his way down to Egypt and was bought by Potiphar, an Egyptian who was one of Pharaoh's officials. Over and over throughout Joseph's life, we see "the Lord was with Joseph and he prospered" (Gen. 39:2). It was so evident that Potiphar took notice: "When his master saw that the Lord was with him and that the Lord gave him success in everything he did, Joseph found favor in his eyes and became his attendant" (Gen. 39:3-4).

There's a valuable lesson to learn to find the key for Joseph's success—"the Lord was with him." You may say, "I don't feel very successful right now. My life is actually a mess. My husband has been out of work for months, and we're depleting our savings just trying to survive from month to month." Or it could be you have a surgery on the horizon—the doctor isn't sure if it is cancer, but they won't know until they go in. Maybe it's your son or daughter who is a prodigal and they've strayed from God and it is a great sorrow for you. In all of our heartaches we must believe by faith that God is with us. The Lord promised us, "I am with you always, even to the end of the age" (Matt. 28:20). "Never will I leave you; never will I forsake you" (Heb. 13:5). Even though Joseph found favor and the Lord was with him, He was still a slave in a foreign country far from his father. We have to remember that this world is not our home. We are living in a foreign land, so to speak. Our home is in heaven, and we're only here for a very short time when comparing it to eternity. One day very soon we will see clearly, for now we see in a mirror dimly. And on that day we will be reunited with our heavenly Father and beloved Jesus.

In addition to Joseph's trials—rejected by his brothers, thrown in a pit and sold into slavery—he was also falsely accused by Potiphar's wife. Read Genesis 39:4-20. Joseph is put in prison: "But while Joseph was there in prison, the Lord was with him; He showed him kindness and granted him favor in the eyes of the prison warden. . . . The warden paid no attention to anything under Joseph's care, because the Lord was with Joseph and gave him success in whatever he did" (Gen. 39:20-21, 23). As we will witness in Joseph's life, the Lord had a plan all along. The Lord is on our side. He loves us supremely. He loved you to death, proving his love for you when Jesus died on the cross to pay the penalty for your sins. We're forgiven because Jesus was forsaken. We're white as snow though our sins were as scarlet. The Lord is faithful and it may not look like things are perfect, but remember your story isn't over. God is not through with you. Just like Joseph's story, there is still much ahead.

"Let us not become weary in doing good, for at

the proper time we will reap a harvest if we do not give up" (Gal. 6:9). Scripture doesn't share Joseph's thoughts or feelings during this time; it's silent. All we know is that during the hardest time of his life, the Lord was with him. For you too it may be one of the hardest trials you've ever faced, but trust in faith that God is with you and that He will be with you to the end. In the next chapter, we will conclude with Joseph. Until then, take your burdens and sorrows and cast them upon the Lord, for he cares for you. Be honest with him about any fears or worries; He already knows.

"Trust in the Lord and do good; dwell in the land and enjoy safe pasture. Delight yourself in the Lord and He will give you the desires of your heart. Commit your way to the Lord; trust in Him and He will do this. . . . Be still before the Lord and wait patiently for him" (Psalm 37:3-7). I love all those verbs: trust, dwell, delight, commit, be still. This is your "to do list" today. Trust God; He is able. Dwell (think) upon His Word, His character, His promises; it will bring you great delight as you ponder who He is. And then commit your way to Him.

"I would have lost heart, unless I had believed that I would see the goodness of the Lord in the land of the living. Wait on the Lord (like a waiter at a restaurant, serve Him); be of good courage, and He shall strengthen your heart; Wait, I say, on the Lord!" (Psalm 27:13-14).

God Meant It for Good

But as for you, you meant evil
against me; but God meant it for good,
in order to bring it about as it is this day,
to save many people alive.
Genesis 50:20

Chapter 3

When we left off in the last chapter, Joseph was still a slave, still in prison, still separated from his beloved father and brother Benjamin whom he loved deeply. Today may find you in the same trial you were in yesterday, your circumstances haven't changed; but I do hope one thing has changed: your perspective. I hope you are holding on to God's promises and that His very presence is a comfort to you in whatever you're facing. Let's look at God's ultimate plan and purpose in Joseph's life.

Early on in Joseph's story, it was a dream God had given him that sparked envy in his brothers. Perhaps there was an underlying tension in their relationship for years, but Joseph's vision of them "bowing down to him" was too much for them to stomach. God had indeed given Joseph a vision years before and now he's in prison and here comes the Pharaoh's butler and baker. Both men have had dreams and they don't understand the meanings. It is God who gives the interpretation of those dreams to Joseph. It was two full years after the butler was released from prison and restored to his position that Pharaoh had a dream. Not one of his wise men could tell the meaning of his dream. Finally the butler remembered Joseph: "So Pharaoh sent for Joseph" (Gen. 41:14). This is now years after Joseph was sold by his brothers, perhaps thirteen years later. The days had turned to weeks, the weeks into months, and year after year Joseph was there waiting, serving, trusting, and hoping—possibly pondering the vision God had given to him and wondering how it was going to work out. Ultimately, God gives Joseph the meaning of Pharaoh's dream; and, like the best rags to riches story, Joseph goes from slave to second in command of all of Egypt in just one afternoon. Remember Romans 8:28: "And we know that in all things God works for the good of those who love Him, who have been called according to His purpose." All along God was at work, orchestrating the events of Joseph's life for His divine plan. We may not see it now, but God is doing the same for us as well. Keep loving Jesus even though you don't quite see His grand plan. Walk in faith believing that "He who calls you is faithful, who will also do it" (1 Thess. 5:24).

Now Pharaoh's dream revealed a famine that was to come. God revealed to Joseph a plan to prepare and store up grain during the plentiful years of harvest so that there would be enough grain when the famine hit. Here's a life lesson for us: when you find yourself in the calm before the storm, that's the time to prepare—to store up the manna of His Word in your heart—so that when the famine comes you're well stocked with the provision of God's promises to carry you through the storm.

Fast forward and Joseph is now thirty years old (Gen. 41:46). As he begins his service under Pharaoh, he's given a wife; and within a few years time he has two sons. One son is named Manasseh (Gen. 41:51). The second son is named Ephraim: "For God has caused me to be fruitful in the land of my affliction" (Gen. 41:52). For years, Joseph had suffered. First the loss of his family; second the loss of his home; third the loss of his mother; fourth the heartache of all that his brothers put him through. But now, years later, there's fruitfulness! Amazingly, he's been restored, rescued, released and blessed by God. Jumping ahead a few chapters we find Joseph's brothers making their way down to Egypt during the time of famine. It's now nine years later. Seven years of plentiful crops have passed and it's the second year of famine with five more years to go (Gen. 42-45). The brothers of Joseph come for grain, and in the end Joseph finally reveals himself to them. Remember he's now twenty years older. He's a man, not the boy they rejected. Most likely, Joseph looked very different as well— dressed in Egyptian attire and speaking a foreign language. His identity had been completely concealed to them. "I am Joseph your brother, whom you sold into Egypt. But now, do not therefore be grieved or angry with yourselves because you sold me here; for God sent me before you to preserve life. . . . And God sent me before you to preserve posterity for you in the earth, and to save your lives by a great deliverance. So now it was not you who sent me here, but God" (Gen. 45:4-5, 7-8). At the time, the brothers didn't know they were sending him to Egypt, but God did. It wasn't until twenty years later that Joseph could see the full picture and reason for all he suffered and endured. His vision had been fulfilled, the brothers did eventually "bow down to him" and in God's sovereignty His will was accomplished. Joseph was there, right where God wanted him, to save a nation and to save a family.

I can't help but think of Jesus, the Savior of the world, the Savior of nations, of every tongue and tribe. Jesus was sent from heaven above with the sole mission to save mankind, nations, families and individuals. God had a plan for the Children of Israel as a nation. But He also had a plan for Joseph personally, to make him fruitful in the land of his affliction. Fruitful speaks of being productive, plenteous and life-giving. And yet the fruit of the Spirit is love. When we look upon Joseph's life, we see God's love produced in and through him. A love that forgave his brothers. A love that was patient and kind. A love that truly suffered long. His love was not boastful in his position as second in command of Egypt. His love wasn't proud or haughty. His love was not rude and certainly did not keep a record of being wronged. Just as true *agape* love, God's love always protects, trusts, hopes and perseveres (1 Cor. 13:7). What better example do we see than of Joseph genuinely loving his family by protecting them in the famine, trusting God to see him through, hoping in the vision God had given him and persevering in the

13

midst of a twenty-year ordeal?

I too can testify to God's faithfulness. It's been twenty years since I first stepped out on the mission field as a single woman, not knowing what the Lord had in store for me. During those twenty years, the Lord gave me a loving husband and three wonderful children. In that span of time there have been sorrows, deaths, heartaches, times of grieving and hurtful tears. But oh the joys of my Jesus being at my side with me every step of the way, there to guide me and comfort me. His Word has sustained me, His Spirit has continually filled me through it all, and He has been oh so very faithful to work it all for good. Dear sister, I pray that whatever comes your way, God will work that same *agape* love in you. May we, too, be productive, having God's love produced in us. God is love. Love is the direct result of abiding in Jesus. Love comes from God, plain and simple. No matter what we face may we, like Joseph, trust the Lord with eyes of faith and know that what was meant for evil God can turn around for good—and in the process make us vessels filled with His love.

"The Lord is good, a stronghold in the day of trouble; and He knows those who trust in Him" (Nahum 1:7).

Free Indeed

Whom the Son sets free is free indeed.
John 8:36

Chapter 4

Within these eight words is a rich goldmine. Let's go mining for gold. First we need to answer a few questions: Whose Son is able to set us free? What did He set us free from? When did He set us free? Why did He set us free? And how did He set us free?

"For God so loved the world, that He gave his only begotten Son, that whosoever believes in Him should not perish, but have everlasting life" (John 3:16). Whose Son claims to set us free? God's Son. Only Jesus can offer genuine freedom. He alone is the Way, the Truth and the Life. Jesus came for this very purpose. "He has sent Me to heal the brokenhearted, to proclaim liberty to the captives, and the opening of the prison to those who are bound" (Isaiah 61:1).

Noah Webster defines *free* as "being at liberty; to rescue or release from slavery, captivity or confinement; to loose." Synonyms for *free* include liberation, redemption, deliverance, salvation and come to the rescue. "Deliverance is of the Lord" (Prov. 21:31). "In Him we have redemption through His blood, the forgiveness of sins, according to the riches of His grace" (Eph. 1:7). "Salvation belongs to the Lord" (Ps. 3:8). It's Jesus who saves. He has come to our rescue. Other synonyms for *free* are unchained, unshackled, released and unbound.

Freedom is something we take for granted living in a free country, as opposed to growing up in a Communist country where certain liberties are taken away. As a citizen of the United States of America I am born with God-given rights, all of which are written in the Constitution. One of those rights is the freedom to worship God and go to a church where His Word is taught. There is freedom to proclaim his good news openly and without fear of persecution.

Second, what am I freed from? For the Christian, freedom is on a spiritual level. To be free implies I was once a slave to sin or in slavery to my flesh. Before Christ, we were in bondage to our sin nature. The yoke of its constraint caused all of us to fall prey to the lust of our flesh. We have all had to recognize we were under the control of and enslaved to our sin nature when we came to Christ. He alone has been able to truly set us free. "But now having been set free from sin, and having become slaves of God, you have your fruit to holiness, and the end, everlasting life" (Rom. 6:22). What did the Son do to give us this freedom? He who knew no sin became sin for us. "Not with the blood of goats and calves, but with His own blood He entered the Most Holy Place once for all, having obtained eternal redemption" (Heb. 9:12).

When did the Son set me free? When he died on Calvary. When he willingly laid down his life at the cross. He became that sacrificial lamb. "Knowing that you were not redeemed with corruptible things, like silver or gold, from your aimless conduct received by tradition from your fathers, but with the precious blood of Christ, as of a lamb without blemish and without spot" (1 Peter 1:18-19).

Why did the Son do all this? Why would Jesus choose to die for you and for me? Because He loves us and desires that we live fruitful lives. "Jesus loves me this I know, for the Bible tells me so." He knew there was no other way to free my life from the penalty of sin. "For all have sinned and fall short of the glory of God" (Rom. 3:23). "For the wages of sin is death, but the gift of God is eternal life in Christ Jesus our Lord" (Rom. 6:23). The great joy of coming to Jesus is liberation. I've been released from the grip that the enemy had on my life and I am now free to live for Him and bear fruit for Him.

How did all this happen? The blood of Jesus has atoned for our sin and the chains that once held us captive have been loosed. Where we were once prisoners of sin and Satan, now we serve a new master. We have become a slave unto righteousness (Rom. 6:18)—a slave by choice. Jesus gives us a yoke that is easy and a burden that is light. With this new freedom, I have rest for my soul. "Nor is there salvation in any other, for there is no other name under heaven given among men by which we must be saved" (Acts 4:12).

Have you been set free from the bondage of sin? If yes, praise the Lord. "Stand fast therefore in the liberty by which Christ has made us free, and do not entangled again with a yoke of bondage" (Gal. 5:1). If not, come to Jesus. He loves you so very much. He longs to set you free. Prisons come in all shapes and sizes. You don't necessarily have to be behind physical bars to be a captive. And not all captivity is because of sin. Fear is often the greatest prison. It holds us back, keeps us enslaved by the enemy and keeps us from living a fruitful life. May God's perfect love cast out all fear from your heart. May you hear His still small whisper, "Fear not, for I am with you; be not dismayed, for I am your God. I will strengthen you, yes, I will help you, I will uphold you with My righteous right hand" (Isaiah 41:10). Maybe your prison is grief. You've suffered the death of a loved one, a parent or spouse who had died because of cancer and the grief is unbearable. Or possibly your grief is due to a child who suddenly passed away in a terrible accident. Jesus came "to comfort all who mourn, to console those who mourn in Zion, to give them beauty for ashes, the oil of joy for mourning, the garment of praise for the spirit of heaviness; that they may be called the trees of righteousness, the planting of the Lord, that He may be glorified" (Isaiah 61:3).

As women, so much of who we are revolves around our emotions. Yet we are called to walk by faith and not by our emotions. If you struggle with depression and it has you burdened, look unto Jesus; fix your eyes on Him. Think upon those things that are good, pure, and praiseworthy. I encourage you to go through the ABCs and find an attribute of God's character for each letter. You can also make a list of things to be thankful for as well. For example, *A*—He is altogether lovely. I'm accepted in the Beloved. *B*—

He is My Beloved. He's given me all spiritual blessings in Christ Jesus. C—He is Christ. He chose me. I'm so grateful. I trust that when you do that, you will see Jesus for who He is: your salvation, liberation, deliverer, redeemer and rescuer. He longs to be to us all this and so much more. Titus 2:11 & 14: "For the grace of God that brings salvation has appeared to all men . . . who gave himself for us, that He might redeem us from every lawless deed and purify for himself His own special people, zealous for good works." Celebrate your salvation and the grace of God. May you be "filled with the fruits of righteousness which are by Jesus Christ, to the glory and praise of God" (Phil. 1:11).

Through Many Hardships

Strengthening the disciples
and encouraging them to remain true
to the faith. "We must go through
many hardships to enter
the kingdom of God."
Acts 14:22

Chapter 5

A few verses before this, Paul is stoned and left for dead. Amazingly he gets up and makes his way back to the city. The next day he and Barnabas leave for Derbe. Paul continues on steadfast, immovable, on course, set to his task and goal. His mission: "to strengthen the disciples and encourage them to remain true to the faith." Now I've never faced stoning or been left for dead. I have been in pain after waking up from surgery and, I'll be honest, the next day I hardly felt like going anywhere. Paul amazes me! I couldn't imagine getting out of bed much less walking back to a city where I was stoned. How does he do that? What compels him? His Savior, Jesus Christ. Paul's life was so altered when he came to the Lord and was converted on the Damascus Road (Acts 9). The Spirit of God filled him and immediately Paul surrendered his life. He was never the same, a miraculous transformation took place.

As we look around our world today we see so many people in crisis. People are losing their homes. There are prodigal sons and daughters who have strayed away from the faith. It is tragic when, even in the church, unfaithful spouses are tearing their families apart through divorce. And then there are illnesses that plague our country, families and children. Where does it all end? How do we go on? We all have our hardships, but like Paul we need to choose to move forward and go *through* them. The promise above does have a silver lining. It doesn't say that we are to remain in our trials. No, it says we will go *through* them to enter the kingdom of God. "There will be a day, no more tears, no more pain." This quote is from a line in a song that Jeremy Camp sings about heaven. It's going to happen, one day, and I can hardly wait.

One of my favorite promises is Isaiah 43:1-2: "Fear not, for I have redeemed you; I have called you by your name; you are Mine. When you pass *through* the waters, I will be with you; and *through* the rivers, they shall not overflow you." It may seem impossible to get through the hardship you are in, but take courage. You will go *through* it. And you will come out the other side of it with greater faith, more compassion and most importantly a deeper walk with God. That's what being *fruitful in affliction* is all about. The Lord will not leave you stranded or let you drown. He was faithful to his disciples when they were caught in a raging storm. Mark 4:35-41, take the time to read it. Jesus came into their storm, into their trial. The waves that beat upon their boat and caused them to be full of fear were stilled by three simple words, "Peace, be still" (Mark 4:39). I just love that. May Jesus speak his words of peace and comfort over you, even now in your personal storm. Be still and know that He is God. He is able to calm the waters. "O Lord God of Hosts, who is mighty like You, O Lord? Your faithfulness also surrounds You. You rule the raging of the sea; when its waves rise, You still them" (Ps. 89:8-9). Have you ever felt like you were drowning? The situation becomes unbearable and you feel like, "This is it. I'm going under, it's over." The enemy would love to paint the blackest, bleakest picture he can and keep us enslaved to fear. Jesus didn't leave his disciples in their storm to drown. He rescued them. You have to read on to the next chapter to see their rescue. "Then they came to the other side of the sea . . ." (Mark 5:1). They made it to the other side and so will we.

Back to Paul, he didn't give up and throw a pity party. He didn't get focused on himself which can be our tendency. He remained kingdom focused. His eyes were on the prize—heaven. He sought to share the good news with as many people as he could, to finish the work set before him. His mindset was others first. In this day the saying is so popular, "It's all about me." Well, honestly it's not, and when we think it is, that's our problem. The enemy tries to keep us self-centered; it's a prison, watch out. The next time you find yourself there, search for someone else that you can talk to about *them* and *their* life. Ask them questions about how they are doing and pray for them. Jesus came with a mission in mind, "For even the Son of Man did not come to be served, but to serve, and to give His life a ransom for many" (Mark 10:45). Jesus is our example and pattern for life. Paul lived it out, a man on a mission, driven and filled with the Spirit of God. Rest assured that whatever you're facing, whatever you're going through, you will go through it and Jesus will cross you over to the other side.

Psalm 46:1-3, 5, 10, and 11 says, "God is our refuge and strength, a very present help in trouble. Therefore we will not fear, even though the earth be removed, and though the mountains be carried into the midst of the sea; though its waters roar and be troubled, though the mountains shake with its swelling. . . . God is in the midst of her, she shall not be moved; God shall help her, just at the break of dawn. . . . Be still, and know that I am God. . . . The Lord of Hosts is with us; the God of Jacob is our refuge." Amen! Hallelujah! What a Savior we have.

Even when it looks like our world is crashing down around us, Jesus is right there by our side. The enemy loves to keep us focused on our problems. Be like Paul: forget about yourself, "strengthen the disciples," encourage those around you. The Lord would have us productive and effective in our service for Him; that's the heart of living a fruitful life. To *strengthen* is defined as "to make strong or stronger; to confirm, to establish; to fix in resolution." It can also mean reinforce. If you have a friend who is going through a tough time, pray for her; write her a note with a scripture to encourage her, which will reinforce her faith in God. To *encourage* means "to give courage to; to give or increase confidence of success; to inspire; to incite." Synonyms for encourage include "hearten, cheer, assure, reassure, buoy up, embolden." Moses was told by God in Deuteronomy 3:28, "But commission Joshua, and encourage and strengthen him, for he will lead this people across and will cause them to inherit the land that you will see." Joshua had a huge task before him, he needed to be confirmed in his calling and reassured in what he was about to do. To *encourage* someone can simply mean you offer them hope . . . hope in God; trust . . . trust in the Lord (Prov. 3:5-6); assurance . . . He who began a good work in you will be faithful to complete it (Phil 1:6). I hope you are encouraged . . . pass it on!

If you are the mom of a child with special needs or have a friend with a child who has special needs, let me encourage you to first look to the Lord for He alone is our Hope. That is why Hope Outreach Ministry was created: to REACH OUT to moms and offer them the support and prayer of the body of Christ, to come along side and bear one another's burdens that you too would be *Fruitful in Affliction*. For more information you can contact hopeoutreachirvine@yahoo.com.

The Gift of Grace

Consider Abraham: "He believed God and it was
credited to him as righteousness."
Galatians 3:6

Chapter 6

If you are a believer, you're saved by the simple belief that Jesus died for your sins and rose again. You had nothing to do with it. He did it all on the cross of Calvary. It's a gift. We don't *earn* gifts at Christmas or birthdays, we just *receive* and enjoy them. How much more the gift of salvation, given to us from our heavenly Father who loved us while we were yet sinners? If you have yet to give your life to Christ, simply ask Him to come into your life, confess with your mouth that Jesus is Lord, that he died for your sins and rose from the dead, conquering sin and death for you. "For by grace you have been saved through faith, and that not of yourselves; it is the gift of God, not of works, lest anyone should boast" (Eph. 2:8-9). It's only by God's grace that we can live a life *fruitful in affliction*. We need His grace to make it through the day. Let's explore all His grace affords us.

Grace—it's "free, ready, quick, goodwill, kindness." I love that. God's grace is free of charge and it's available the moment we ask. He's ready and willing, with arms open wide, offering to any and all who wish to come. At any point in the day, I can come to him for more. So many people have this impression of God: that He is an ogre, stingy and grumpy. Nothing could be further from the truth. Our God is the God of all grace (2 Cor. 9:8). He is filled with kindness and goodwill that He longs to extend toward us. He bids us to come to His Throne of Grace boldly "that we may obtain mercy and find grace to help in time of need" (Heb. 4:16).

Second, grace is "appropriately the free, unmerited love and favor of God, the spring and source of all the benefits men receive from him." I love getting a good deal when I'm shopping. This is the best deal out there: the God of heaven and earth, the Creator of the universe, offers us grace, his love and favor freely to us. *Unmerited* means "obtained without service"—I didn't work for it. *Favor* is "to regard with kindness; to support; to aid; God gave Joseph favor and wisdom in the sight of Pharaoh." What could be better than receiving the kindness and love of our Savior? It says in Ephesians 1:3, "Praise be to the God and Father of our Lord Jesus Christ, who has blessed us in the heavenly realms with every spiritual blessing in Christ." A benefit is something that gives me an advantage or support. Benefits are profitable. How many blessings and benefits do we have in Christ? Oh, so many! Just to name a few from Ephesians 1: We have the blessing of being chosen, predestined, adopted, accepted, redeemed, forgiven, and sealed. I encourage you to search for the blessings God has so graciously bestowed upon us as daughters of the King.

Third, grace is "the divine influence or the

influence of the Spirit in renewing the heart and restraining from sin." "My Grace is sufficient" (2 Cor. 12:9). If I want to live a fruitful life as a believer, I need the influence of the Spirit upon my life daily, moment by moment.

Influence literally means "a flowing in, into or on, and referring to substances spiritual or too subtle to be visible, like inspiration." "God hath his influence into the very essence of all things" (Hooker). "In a general sense; influence denotes power whose operation is invisible and known only by its effects, or a power whose cause and operation are unseen." It is the power of the Holy Spirit *upon* my life and His Presence *with* me and *in* me that brings about the fruit of the Spirit. I am saved at the initial place where I put my faith in Jesus as my Lord and Savior. "But you shall receive power when the Holy Spirit has come upon you" (Acts 1:8). When an act of kindness comes forth from a believer, that is the direct outflow of the Spirit working in and through that person. But for there to be "outflow," there must first be an "inflow." Oh, how we need the Holy Spirit filling us on a continual basis as we desire to be fruitful in this life. Jesus said, "I am the vine, you are the branches. He who abides in Me, and I in him, bears much fruit; for without Me you can do nothing" (John 15:5). It's not that I can do *some* things, or handle a *few* things on my plate. No, I can do *nothing* apart from Him. The good news is that as I abide in Him, like a branch staying connected to the vine, the fruit will come naturally. Jesus said, "You did not choose Me, but I chose you and appointed you that you should go and bear much fruit, and that your fruit should remain . . ." (John 15:16). You've been chosen by God himself to bear fruit, lasting fruit that will go on into eternity. Paul said in Philippians 4:13, "I can do all things through Christ who strengthens me." What a difference the Lord makes in our lives—without Him I can do nothing, but with Him all things are possible; victory over fear, love for a difficult person, joy in the midst of sorrow, peace in the storms of life, patience with a challenging child, kindness when we're exhausted beyond our limit. Only then is His goodness, gentleness and self-control evident in our lives.

There's still more of God's grace to discover. We've barely scratched the surface. Fourth, grace is "the application of Christ's righteousness to the sinner." "Where sin abounded, grace did much more abound" (Rom. 5:20). An acrostic for GRACE has been declared: God's Riches At Christ's Expense. Abraham was credited with righteousness because of his belief in God; so, too, for us. We come to God not on our own merit, because truly no good thing dwells within us (Rom. 7:18). We come to God with the belief that on the cross Jesus' righteousness was applied to our account.

"Grace is a state of reconciliation to God." Because of the cross, I am now in harmony with God. There is an agreement with my spirit and His Holy Spirit. The Bible says that prior to coming to Christ I was hostile to God and there were irreconcilable differences between us, namely sin. God is Holy and I'm not by nature. I was born in sin. But through this

28

reconciliation I now have peace of mind and comfort. There's contentment in my soul. It's all because of God's grace.

Lastly, grace can be defined as "eternal life"—the final salvation. "So brace up your minds; be sober (circumspect, morally alert); set your hope wholly and unchangeably on the grace (divine favor) that is coming to you when Jesus Christ (the Messiah) is revealed" (I Peter 1:13). Just as Abraham did, I accept God's Word by faith. Faith can be defined as "an entire confidence or trust in God's character and declarations and in the character and doctrines of Christ with an unreserved surrender to the will of His guidance and dependence on his merits for salvation." It's also "that firm belief of God's testimony and of the truth of the gospel which influences the will and lends to an entire reliance on Christ for salvation."

Abraham put his faith in a reliable person—the maker of heaven and earth. He surrendered "without reservation" his entire life "to the will of his guidance" and followed God, not knowing where he was going; leaving his country in obedience to God's will for his life. Abraham is called the Father of Faith for us who believe. He went on to live quite a fruitful life. Take time to ponder and celebrate this truly, wonderful gift: the grace of God. Continue to trust Him. Look to Him and His grace to sustain you through your day. His grace is enough!

The Helper

Nevertheless I tell you the truth.
It is to your advantage that I go away;
for if I do not go away, the Helper will not
come to you; but if I depart,
I will send Him to you.
John 16:7

Chapter 7

Jesus promised that "when He, the Spirit of truth, has come, He will guide you into all truth; for He will not speak on His own authority, but whatever He hears He will speak; and He will tell you things to come" (John 16:13). The Holy Spirit is the third person of the Trinity. He was there at creation: "The Spirit of God was moving over the surface of the waters" (Genesis 1:2). I like that. God's Spirit *moves* in our lives as well. He is actively involved in my day to day life. And to the extent that I give Him access to my heart, the more fruitful it will become. "For it is God who is at work in you, both to will and to work for His good pleasure" (Phil. 2:13). God has a divine design for your life. He has graciously given to us His Spirit to take up residence within us for His will and good pleasure to be accomplished. We cannot live a productive, active, useful life without His help. If Jesus' life was empowered by the Spirit, how much more do we need Him? "You know of Jesus of Nazareth, how God anointed Him with the Holy Spirit and with power, and how He went about doing good and healing all who were oppressed by the devil, for God was with Him" (Acts 10:38). What a blessing it must have been to all those who came in contact with Jesus. There were those who were spiritually oppressed, physically depressed and emotionally wrecked. Perhaps you fit into one of those categories. Jesus touched so many lives bringing healing, hope and health. He wants to touch your life as well. He went about doing good. And He is our example. Yes, He was fully God but also fully man; remember, He "emptied himself, taking the form of a bond-servant, and being made in the likeness of men" (Phil. 2:7). That same Spirit dwells in us, and so then ought we to live by the Spirit and not according our flesh. "But if the Spirit of Him who raised Jesus from the dead dwells in you, He who raised Christ Jesus from the dead will also give life to your mortal bodies through His Spirit who dwells in you" (Rom. 8:11). "The helper, the Holy Spirit, whom the Father will send in My name, He will teach you all things, and bring to your remembrance all that I said to you" (John 14:26). We are instructed to "be filled with the Spirit" (Eph. 5:18). This is not a onetime filling but a continual filling that takes place every day of our life, maybe even every hour. As we seek to live a life filled with the fruit of the Spirit, it's important we know who is along our side—in us and with us—as we walk with the Lord.

It struck me the other night as I was pondering the

fruit of the Spirit, that little word *of* became larger than life and it is the key that unlocks the door *of* fruitfulness. *Of*: otherwise known as a preposition in grammar (trust me, this is important as we will see). A preposition is used in our language to show a "relationship between its object and some other word in the sentence" (*BJU Grammar*, pg. 142). *Relationship*, that is so interesting. We are in a relationship with Jesus our Savior and beloved Redeemer, who is our "subject" so to speak when we think of our life as a sentence. The Father, Jesus and the Holy Spirit—the triune God becomes the subject of our life when we surrender to Him at conversion. That is the beginning of our new relationship with the Lord. Just as Jesus was baptized, we need the Spirit to come and descend upon us (Luke 3:21-22). *Of:* "the primary sense is departing, issuing or proceeding from; or out of, as the cause, source, means, author or agent bestowing." Another quick grammar lesson: A noun that follows the preposition is the "object of the preposition." The fruit that is evidenced in our lives first precedes from a *relationship* with God the Holy Spirit. The love comes *from* Him. It all *departs* from Him, *into* us. He is the *source, cause, means, author and agent* from which all fruit flows. His love is evidenced in my life by joy, peace, patience, goodness, gentleness, kindness and self-control. This is so very important because I cannot produce fruit on my own. It's the fruit *of* the Spirit.

Knowing the Holy Spirit is vital to my life as a Christian. He is called the helper—a helper is one who aids, assists and supports. Synonyms for *help* are relief, sustain, maintain, nourish, rescue, quicken, uphold, nurture, cultivate, serve, advocate, cheer, encourage, at my beck and call, means, lend a hand, favor, smile upon, cultivate, befriend. The Holy Spirit is all this and so much more. He has a *relief* ministry which is truly supernatural, living in us and equipping us with power to walk in the Father's will and purpose. He *sustains* and *maintains* my life moment by moment, like manna in the wilderness. He is there to *nourish* my soul with the Word of God, giving me understanding and guidance. He has *means*, and His supply is limitless. He's near to *lend a hand* or *take me by the hand* when I need direction. He comes to our *rescue*, knowing exactly what we need. He's *quickened* my life from darkness to light. He *upholds* me by the power of His Word and precious promises. His job is to cultivate more of Jesus in our lives, teaching us and bringing to our minds the Word of God. He is perfectly content to *serve*, to *wait* on and *take care* of me as my helper, this side of heaven. He's my *advocate*. He *sticks up* for me when the enemy attacks. He's there to *cheer* me on when I'm down and *encourage* me when I'm fearful. He *smiles* upon me with *favor* from above. He has befriended me and is at my beck and call.

The Holy Spirit is here in this world for a threefold purpose: to "convict the world of sin, and righteousness, and of judgment (John 16:8-11). We are the vessels that He lives through. "Do you not know that your body is the temple of the Holy Spirit who is in you, whom you have from God, and you are not your own?" (1 Cor. 6:19). He is not only *the helper* but a help practically. He's a blessing, a benefit, a godsend (literally). Help means "to lend strength or means towards effecting a purpose." God's purpose for my life and yours is "Christ in you, the hope of glory" (Col. 1:27). His ministry is to "serve, help, avail, and do good toward the believer." Help speaks of usefulness, availability, being handy, also invaluable. I know I need all the help I can get. Certainly the Holy Spirit is helpful, valuable, and of great worth. He convicts and corrects me when I sin; it's his kindness that leads me to repentance. Jesus said it's to our advantage that He go away, so the Holy Spirit can come to us. He is the one who fills my cup and causes my life to be fruitful. He is available any time, any place. He is ready 24/7—morning, noon, and night; to the husband working late nights or the mom with a newborn baby who is up early or the homeschool mom who cries out for help in the middle of her day, "Help, please!"(That would be me!) He is so very near, "at hand." What a comfort He is. It is totally advantageous to call upon Him. He is a present help in time of need. He's simply invaluable. I cannot live without Him and neither can you. Call upon Him even now, for the strength you need. He is available always. All you need to do is ask. In the next chapter we will learn about the Holy Spirit filling our lives, as we yield to Him.

Bring Forth Much Fruit

Verily, verily, I say unto you, except a corn of wheat fall into the ground and die, it abideth alone: but if it die, it bringeth forth much fruit.
John 12:24

Chapter 8

We've gleaned from God's Word that the fruit He desires in our lives is "of the Spirit." It's not in and of ourselves, but a supernatural work of His Spirit filling us as we abide in Him. In order for Him to fill my life, I must first die, submit, yield and be emptied of self. A full cup has no room to receive anything else. So often our *cup* is filled with our own plans and our flesh—it just needs to be dumped, emptied completely, to make room for something new. In 2 Chronicles 30:8, the Israelites had been invited to keep the Passover by King Hezekiah. "Now be ye not stiff-necked, as your fathers were, but yield yourselves unto the Lord." *Yield* means "to allow, to concede, to permit, to emit, to give up, to resign, to surrender, to comply with, to give way, not to oppose." For the Holy Spirit to fill my cup I must give up, surrender and allow Him to come in and entirely saturate my soul. To yield speaks of something soft, not hard, pliable and flexible. I must be a willing, workable instrument in his hands. I must relax my grip and stay tender to the Lord, as opposed to being hard-hearted, rigid or stubborn like the Israelites were in the past. Otherwise He cannot truly be Lord of my life, bringing forth the fruit He desires. If I choose to be inflexible it will hinder his ability to fill me. This is not a onetime yielding either, but daily—and more often than not, moment by moment. I encourage you, "even so now yield your members servants to righteousness unto holiness" (Rom. 6:19).

Daily you and I have a choice to submit, comply and acquiesce to His lordship. Will we surrender, like Joseph and Abraham, and resign our will for His, laying down our rights? (Let me just say, we really have no rights. We've been bought with the precious blood of Jesus and our lives are not our own.) To *give way* and live *unresisting* implies consent, agreement. "Can two walk together, unless they are agreed?" (Amos 3:3). The obvious answer is no. Another synonym for yield is "acknowledgement" (Prov. 3:5-6). I must come to that place where I simply acknowledge He knows best. His ways are not my ways and I know nothing. I love this quote; Amy Carmichael said it best, "In acceptance lieth peace." Once I yield to His will and *accept* the lot before me; regardless of the pain and possible fear it entails, the peace will flood in. Many times acceptance includes the unknown: Will I be able to keep my home? Pay the bills? Or get over this illness? This is where we walk by faith. Acceptance also includes those things I can't change and frankly didn't ask for or necessarily want in my life. Let's be honest, when it's an illness, or worse yet, the diagnosis of a child that this isn't going to get better this side of heaven, that's where I fully surrender and yield to Him as my loving helper. Yes, I still pray and hope and believe and trust that God is able to do the impossible. Yet some things are final, like a death. And some losses are so painful to accept it is only with God's help and filling that we can have victory and be fruitful in affliction. In those times we look to Him to give us hope and empower us to run our course.

The opposite of *yield* is refuse, reject, protest or resist, flat out or point blank. Do I at times protest in my flesh and resist Him? Am I deaf to His still small voice? Am I ever "non-compliant or unconsenting" to Him? He will only take us as far as we are willing to go. A child in a mother's arms might feel safe in the shallow end, but once she ventures out into the deep end that child can resist and squirm and kick. The Holy Spirit is a gentleman; He will not force the Father's will upon us. He is here to embolden us, to fulfill the Father's good pleasure in and through our lives. Far be it for me to ever say, "*Not on your life* am I doing that, or going there". In our flesh those thoughts can pop up. That is why it is so important to be filled with His holiness and not walking in the flesh, according to our sinful nature. Our plans, agendas and ideas of how it's all supposed to be must be surrendered, relinquished, let go and abandoned. It's a choice we make to give way, to part with, and lay aside our will for His, just as Jesus prayed, "Not my will be done, but Thy will." If I seek to keep my life, I will lose it. But if I die like that grain of seed, I will become fruitful and flourish. Give notice to your flesh: it's God's way, nothing less, nothing else.

The blessing in yielding to God is it *YIELDS* heavenly dividends for all of eternity. Just as the children of Israel "sowed fields and planted vineyards that yielded a fruitful harvest" (Ps. 107:37), so too will we be fruitful when we sow to the Spirit. If we choose to sow to the Spirit, we will of the Spirit reap everlasting life (Gal. 6:8). The love that is shared, the acts of kindness that are shown; if you give even a cup of cold water to one of these little ones, it does not go unnoticed. There is eternal value, a prize awaiting us in heaven. Have you ever received a Christmas bonus? Well, we have a heavenly bonus laid up for us in heaven. It's not just an extra check to pay bills or buy gifts that is a onetime deal. And it's way better than a $10 coupon to In-N-Out Burger, although those are nice. This bonus is a treasure beyond imagination that will not rust or decay.

Lastly, being yielded implies "ease, smoothness, a cinch, a snap, child's play." What's one of the all-time favorite things that kids enjoy playing with? Playdough! Why? That's simple: it's soft and pliable, you can make anything out of it, and it's a snap. Playdough doesn't resist the hand of the builder. When we yield to God's filling, we become unburdened and unencumbered with the weight of the world and we are then "strengthened with all might, according to His glorious power" (Col.1:11). May the Holy Spirit have total access to our hearts. May we not hinder or interrupt the flow of His power, peace or presence.

Yesterday at church we concluded Chapter 28 in

the Book of Acts. I loved what my pastor had to say. Although the title of the book is "The Acts of the Apostles" he suggested it could also be called "The Acts *of* the Holy Spirit." (There's that little word again: *of*.) "The book doesn't end with Chapter 28, it continues on with chapter 29 in our lives" (Terry Walker). That is so true. The book isn't finished, the story is still being written in your life and mine. The Holy Spirit is still on the move, still looking for those He can fill and equip and bring forth fruit in. He still desires to act on our behalf; may we invite Him to have his way.

Don't be afraid to die to your hopes and dreams, to empty the *cup* of your plans. I've learned as I've surrendered my life to the Lord that He's the One who fills my cup to overflowing. Pastor Chuck has taught this lesson about trials: we can grow bitter or better. The choice is ours. I've sought to grow better in my trials with Grace Ann and with the fibromyalgia pain I live with on a daily basis. I want to trust the Lord and keep an eternal perspective. A friend said many years ago the trials we go through are "an opportunity to trust the Lord," knowing He alone can bring beauty from ashes (Isa. 61:3). I had no idea at the brink of tragedy in my life that just around the corner the Lord was writing a new chapter. It was a chapter that included new dreams and plans which made the process of dying a little sweeter.

Filled with the Spirit

Be filled with the Spirit.
Ephesians 5:18

Chapter 9

The Holy Spirit is here with us, sent from the Father to be our helper in this life. He is with us at salvation, and He also comes upon us for empowering. "But you shall receive power (ability, efficiency, and might) when the Holy Spirit has come upon you, and you shall be My witnesses in Jerusalem and all Judea and Samaria and to the ends (the very bounds) of the earth" (Acts 1:8). For Him to fill us we must yield to Him and be emptied of self. We all make choices each day. What will I fill my life and soul with? Here we are instructed to be filled with the Spirit, with God himself, the third person of the Trinity. What could be better? His love is limitless, His patience never runs out, His joy is contagious and it's Him we so desperately need in this world.

Fill: "to put or pour in, till the thing will hold no more; to supply with abundance; to cause to abound; to satisfy; to content; to make full; to occupy; to complete; fullness."

When the Holy Spirit came to take up residence in our hearts at conversion, we became *complete* in Christ. "And you are in Him, made full and having come to fullness of life [in Christ you too are filled with the Godhead—Father, Son and Holy Spirit—and reach full spiritual stature]" (Col. 2:10). "I came that you may have and enjoy life, and have it in abundance (to the full, till it overflows)" (John 10:10). He desires to occupy our hearts and minds and fill every inch within us. May we look to Him—and Him alone—to permeate our lives, which will ultimately satisfy us. If we desire to live an abundant, fruitful life, it begins daily with being filled with the Holy Spirit so that we can live and walk by the Spirit.

"It is the Spirit Who gives life" (John 6:63). How does the Spirit fill me, practically speaking? He does so as I take the time to sit before the Lord, while I'm in the Word, "under the spout where the blessings run out." How do you fill your car up with gas? You park and turn off the engine. It's quite difficult to fill a moving vessel. That's not to say the Lord doesn't refill us as we are on the move serving Him. But we must first take time to wait on Him. The Lord desires to pour himself into our hearts so we are so full that we overflow with His presence. Think of Thanksgiving dinner and all the delicious things you eat at that meal: turkey, mashed potatoes, sweet potatoes, cranberries, rolls—and you must leave room for dessert, too. After dinner you are completely satisfied and the thought of ever eating again is not necessary for a week! We have all felt that way. When are we content? When we are full? I believe there is a spiritual parallel between being filled with the Spirit and being content in the Lord. If I'm full of Him, I don't crave the things of the world. The things that used to pull at me no longer do, because I'm abundantly satisfied by God himself dwelling in me. The question is: "Am I spending enough time with Him to be properly filled?" Since we were created by God and for God, it seems that He alone can satisfy and supply what my soul truly craves.

Fill speaks of completeness, entirety, saturation, totality, brimful, absolute, occupy, presence, occupancy, inhabit, dwell, reside, stay, live, abide, permeate. To *dwell* means to "stay, abide, remain, to abide as a permanent resident; residence for life."

Once the Holy Spirit comes and takes up residence in us, He's here to stay. His ministry is fourfold. In John 16:12-15 it says He is here to "guide us into all truth." Second, He does not speak on His own authority, but whatever He hears He will speak. Third, He will tell us things to come. And fourth, He will glorify Jesus. "He will take of what is Mine and declare it to you." He does this personally, tenderly and with so much compassion. Romans 8:26 says the Spirit is there to help in our weakness. I am personally so thankful that I can look to Him on this heaven-bound journey as He abides with me. Where do I find this satisfaction and joy? "You have made known to me the path of life; you will fill me with joy in your presence, with eternal pleasures at your right hand" (Ps. 16:11). As we come in His presence each and every day, He will faithfully fill and permeate our lives.

Paul prayed in Ephesians 3:16-17, "I pray that out of his glorious riches he may strengthen you with *power* through his Spirit in your inner being, so that

Christ may dwell in your hearts through faith." Why do I need to be filled? It's the power *of* the Holy Spirit, which we so desperately need to live a fruitful life. Power is "the quality which enables individuals to achieve their aims. Scripture stresses the power of God, demonstrated in Jesus Christ's resurrection and bestowed through the Holy Spirit. Scripture also stresses the relative powerlessness of humanity in God's sight" (*Zondervan Dictionary of Biblical Themes*). Power is also defined as "strength, energy, influence, authority, sway, command." We all need to be strengthened and influenced by the Holy Spirit continually.

Synonyms for power are "almightiness, omnipotence, influence, capability, magnetic, productive, and competent." They all point to the person of the Holy Spirit. Jesus was a magnetic personality because his life overflowed with the Spirit. He continually drew people unto himself. Why? He was so loving, kind, caring, forgiving, gentle, helpful, capable and competent. He was fully Man and yet fully God.

P—Our *position:* Are you plugged into the power source? My husband loves those plug-in room fragrances. They really do work and with no effort on my part. I just plug them into the outlet and continually get comments when people come over, "Your home smells so good." Isn't the same true of our lives that if we are plugged in to the Spirit, the source of power, we will be a sweet fragrance unto the world?

O—Are you *occupied* with the Holy Spirit? We

tend to think of being occupied in our mind with our thoughts or with our time. Think of it this way: You're on an airplane and the lavatory has a sign on the door—*vacancy*—when it is not being used. Once you step in, you slide the lock in place and the sign now reads *occupied* on the outside because you have stepped in and the room is in use. We are the temple of the Spirit in which He dwells (1 Cor. 6:19). One of the pastors at my church wrote this in our bulletin and I think it is so appropriate: "When we celebrate Christmas we celebrate more than the birth of Christ and the forgiveness of sin. We celebrate the day God came to fill us with the glory of the Lord" (Charlie Hill).

W—Welcome Him in. We need to invite the Holy Spirit daily to *occupy* our lives. To step in, fill us, and use us. If we are left vacant of His power, there is nothing we can do apart from Him. But when His power is upon us, He will achieve great things through us.

E—Everyday and every moment of the day. Back to our car analogy: If we want to go somewhere, there must be gas in the car. You can't drive around on an empty tank. In our "hurry up" society we can so easily get caught up in going, and even serving, that we forget to just rest and take a Sabbath. There was a popular worship song we used to sing years ago, "Everyday I look to you, to be the strength of my life. You're the Hope I hold on to, to be the strength of my life. . . . Be the strength of my life today." May you look to Him and His abundant supply to give you the strength you need today, one day at a time.

R—"*Remain* in me, and I will remain in you. No branch can bear fruit by itself; it must remain in the vine. Neither can you bear fruit unless you remain in me" (John 15:4). The antonym for power is powerless. It means "destitute of power, force or energy; weak, impotent, not able to produce any effect." That's us without the Holy Spirit. Remember the Holy Spirit is a permanent resident in our life. He has come to dwell, abide in and empower us.

When is a sponge useful? When it's brought under the faucet, immersed under the water and squeezed out. A dry sponge won't get the work done. But a sponge that has been saturated and damp is quite useful altogether. "God is able to make all grace abound toward you; that you, always having all sufficiency in all things, may abound to every good work" (2 Cor. 9:8). The Holy Spirit has the ministry of pouring himself—His power—into our lives, causing us to abound in every good work. God's grace is like a fountain whose source never runs out, make sure you tap into it today. May He occupy you and fill you with the fullness of His presence causing you to spill over to those around you. May He also take possession of your life and employ you for his service.

Living by the Spirit

*But those who live in accordance with the
Spirit have their minds set on what the Spirit
desires. The mind of sinful man is death, but the
mind controlled by the Spirit is life and peace.*
Romans 8:5-6

Chapter 10

To live in and by the Spirit is a daily exercise—day in and day out. Our whole existence, our life and breath, are wrapped up in Him. He is not a *part* of my life, but He is my *whole* life. According to Acts 17:28, "In Him we live and move and have our being." Since coming to God, He has quickened our spirit from death to life. He has literally "put life into us" by His Spirit. As we desire to grow in fruitfulness, filled with His Spirit, we must stand fixed upon His Word and be open to the moving of His Spirit. Our lives are anchored to Him. Thankfully He is there for us to rely on and look to throughout the day. His power is available to help us say yes to God and no to our flesh.

Each one of us is in a race called life. And we all run to win. We don't sprint at full speed from the start if we want to finish well. This is not a 100-yard dash. Life is a marathon. We cannot hurry through in our own efforts and expect to live a fruitful life. We

would eventually burn out and run out of energy,
crashing on the sidelines of life. Our Christian life is
called a *walk*. Walking is simply one step in front of
the other. When you're little like a child, your steps
are small and often slower than an adult. We live in a
fast-paced society that thinks "drive thru" is the norm.
Living by the Spirit means it's one step at a time. It's a
walk. My behavior, conduct, manner and course of
life are all centered around the aim of pleasing Jesus—
to be holy as He is holy, to be loving because He is
loving. And from that love which flows from His
Spirit into our lives, the result is: the joy we find living
in His presence, the peace that only God can give,
patience with others, kindness, gentleness and self-
control. As we grow in our relationship with the Lord
and learn from Him, relinquishing our control, He
shapes our course. He transforms us. It's Christ in us,
the hope of glory (2 Cor. 5:14-15). It really comes
down to daily making the choice to no longer live for
myself but to live for Him. Allow His Spirit to
permeate your life, to take control. He will fill you
and enable you to do the impossible. You are a
citizen of heaven, residing in a foreign land as a
pilgrim. You are just passing through. Make walking
with Him step by step your priority. All you have to
do is place one foot in front of the other as you abide
in Him. As you show up each morning looking to
Him, He will do the rest.

"You are of God, little children, and have
overcome them, because He who is in you is greater
than he who is in the world" (I John 4:4). The good
news of this verse is that God's Spirit is greater than

the enemy we face in this world. Yes, we contend with a clever foe, but he has been defeated at the cross by the blood of Jesus. When Jesus died, he conquered sin, death and Satan. Living in the Spirit also implies that we're not walking in the flesh according to our old sinful nature. Victory has been given. We don't have to give in to our flesh and sin because we are without the power to live victoriously. "Those controlled by the sinful nature cannot please God" (Rom. 8:8). Verse 9 goes on to say, "You, however, are controlled not by the sinful nature but by the Spirit, if the Spirit of God lives in you." Amen! We have access to the power of God's Spirit—tap into it and discover the joy of victory through Jesus.

"If we live in the Spirit, let us also walk in the Spirit" (Gal. 5:25). The Holy Spirit is here to help us as we walk in this world. Fruitfulness is the result of a life filled and flooded with the Spirit. He can shower each of us with peace that passes our understanding in the midst of a fiery trial. He is able to fill our hearts with love for someone who has betrayed us. He can give us patience with a child when our patience has run out. We are His workmanship created in Christ Jesus for good works. He desires our lives to be a harvest of His love that others can glean and benefit from. What's the best thing about fruit? You get to enjoy it and eat it. Whether it's a perfect peach or the most amazing watermelon, it's the sweetness that we're after. May those around us see the love of God in our lives and glorify Him. "And now abide faith, hope, love, these three; but the greatest of these is love" (1 Cor. 13:13).

Greater can also mean mightier, superiority, primacy, pre-eminence, outrank, surpass, outmatch, eclipse, predominate, supreme, the utmost, matchless, foremost, excellent, unrivaled, unparalleled, beyond, unequaled, unsurpassed, incomparable. Our Jesus has won. He is victorious and greater than our foe. The enemy is no match for our Lord; he is inferior in every way and simply falls short. Jesus is absolutely mighty. He has outranked him and eclipsed him by His love and grace. As we live by His Spirit, His divine power is afforded to us. He has given us everything we need for life and godliness (2 Peter 1:3-4). His supply will never run dry (Phil. 4:19).

Think of the supply of the Spirit. *Supply* speaks of resources, provision, to furnish, replenish, fill, and feed. It's to give, bestow, impart, confer, present, furnish, and lavish. Also to store, spring forth like a well, a reserve, or treasure. It speaks of sufficiency, adequacy, being enough, abundance, plentitude, showered down, poured in, absolutely inexhaustible. The resources of God's Spirit are beyond what we can imagine. He gives strength to the weary. He fills the thirsty and needy. He's quick to impart wisdom when we ask. He bestows upon us His favor and lavishes us with His love. His grace is enough for whatever your need is today. "God is able to make all grace abound to you, so that in all things at all times, having all that you need, you will abound in every good work" (2 Cor. 9:8).

Personally, I'm so thankful for the Lord's help as I walk day by day with Him. I have friends who have run marathons and I'm amazed at their stamina. I joke that I can barely run to my mailbox, but it's true. There are days I can hardly move to get out of bed, only to spend the rest of the day on the couch because the pain keeps me horizontal. Standing up for a song at church is not always easy, and sometimes I just can't stand. Yet the Lord has been faithful to stand with me as He stood with Paul (Acts 27:23). He supplies strength and power when I need it. When a group of us from church went on a missions trip to Hungary, I thought, "I'll never be able to keep up with everyone; I'm the weakest link." But the Lord supplied His might on my behalf.

Sometimes, before I get out of bed in the morning, I pray, "Spirit of the Living God, fall afresh on me." And He always meets me, day in and day out. I may not be able to physically run a marathon, but I know with each step I take here on earth I'm getting closer to the finish line of Heaven. Lord willing, the fruit will come as I abide in Him.

"And if the Spirit of Him who raised Jesus from the dead is living in you, He who raised Christ from the dead will also give life to your mortal bodies through His Spirit, who lives in you" (Romans 8:11).

Fragrance of Christ

*For we are to God the fragrance of Christ
among those who are being saved and
among those who are perishing.*
2 Corinthians 2:15

Chapter 11

Would you say your life is marked with the fragrance of Christ, or is it more like an odor? Recently, my nine-year-old daughter got into some perfume of mine and I could smell her fragrance down the hall from the other room. It was absolutely undeniable what she had done. I asked her, "What did you get into?" "Nothing," she quickly told me. And then she confessed, "Only three squirts." She tried to assure me it wasn't that bad, but boy was she potent. And her fragrance continued to linger for quite a while afterward.

A fragrance can be a sweet aroma or a scent. Most often it's pleasant. I have a friend at church who always has a sweet fragrance as she passes me. I love getting a whiff of her perfume—it is such a delight. When I think of fresh fruit, nothing compares to fresh peaches or pineapple. For fruit to reach maturity it needs to hang upon the branch and stay connected to the tree. Fruit depends on the tree getting the proper water and nutrients for it to grow. We've learned that fruit comes directly from abiding in the Lord and it is a result of the Holy Spirit filling us and developing the character of God in our lives. What is the fragrance of Christ? Love! Jesus said, "A new command I give you: Love one another. As I have loved you, so you must love one another. By this all men will know that you are my disciples, if you love one another" (John 13:34-35).

God's love is all things sweet. His love is "patient and kind. It does not envy, it does not boast, it is not proud. It is not rude, it is not self-seeking, it is not easily angered, it keeps no record of wrongs" (1 Cor. 13:4-5). Odors, on the other hand, are not always pleasant and, honestly, some can be downright offensive. As soon as I catch the faintest whiff of a skunk, I batten down the hatches of my home. I quickly close every window because I don't want that stench in my house.

God's love is simply kind. *Kind* is "disposed to do good to others and to make them happy." When we do something kind for another person, they are blessed. As He lavishes us with His loving-kindness we are blessed indeed. *Kind* is also "tenderness or goodness of nature." We know only God is truly good in nature. What a blessing that we can be His vessels through which His love flows to the world around us. Another attribute of God's love revealed under the umbrella of kindness is benevolence or "charitableness, an act of kindness, charity given, good done." Are we to be kind only to those that are kind to us? No, God is kind to the unthankful (Luke 6). We are told in Ephesians 4:32, "Be kind one to another"—a verse I am continually telling my kids when they are not being kind! This love that contributes to the happiness of others is evidenced in the acts that it displays. Love is a verb, thereby demanding action. Synonyms for *kind* are "God's grace, good will, Christian charity, unselfishness, friendship, consideration, practice the golden rule, and do as you would be done by." Aren't all these characteristics of Jesus who is always kind? He is the best friend that sticks closer than a brother, completely and entirely unselfish. He gave us the Golden Rule: Do unto others as you would have them do unto you (Matt. 7:12). Friendships are built on a mutual kindness that is give and take. Why were so many drawn to Jesus? He was loving, kind and friendly. You can place Jesus' name in 1 Corinthians 13 every time the word *love* is written and He fits perfectly.

The greatest act of goodwill in all of history is told of in Titus 3:4-5: "But when the kindness and love of God our Savior appeared, He saved us, not because of righteous things we had done, but because of His mercy." Has anyone ever done anything kinder for you than to die for you? Jesus purchased our salvation when He willingly laid down His life for us. "Greater love has no one than this, that he lay down his life for his friends" (John 15:13).

"Love envies not"—envy speaks of discontent, uneasiness at another's prosperity. Envy springs from pride; it's mortified that another has obtained what one has. It bears ill will toward others. This is not a fragrance we want to wear as daughters of the King.

Envy is an odor, just as boasting is. Love does not boast, it does not flaunt itself. The King James Bible uses the word *vaunteth* instead of *boast*. It's not a word we commonly use today but it means "to brag, to make a vain display of one's' own worth, what one is or has or has done." All that we are in Christ is because of Him. There is no good thing within us apart from him. That's why it is absolutely essential that we stay connected to Him if we want our lives to be fruitful. We have nothing to brag about, every good and perfect gift is from above, every talent or ability that is in our life is from God and Him alone (James 1:17).

Love on the other hand doesn't boast but is humble, meek, lowly, resigned, submitted. Our precious Jesus said of himself, "I am gentle and lowly in heart," when He invited us: "Come to Me, all you who labor and are heavy laden, and I will give you rest. Take My yoke upon you and learn from Me . . . and you will find rest for your souls. For My yoke is easy and My burden is light" (Matt. 11:28-30). Jesus is the best example of God's love. He was continually submitted to His Father's will, surrendered to the cross, lowly in comparison to the Pharisees and perfectly meek. We see Jesus, clothed in humility, on bended knees as He prayed in Gethsemane, "Not as I will, but as You will" (Matt. 26:39). He's clearly a pattern for us to model our lives after; never boasting in himself, "Look what I did," and not puffed up with pretense.

I desire to be one of those vessels through which God's love can flow to others. I think one of the greatest challenges is to love when you're in pain, whether it is physical or emotional. A few years ago I had my seventh surgery. I've had a C-section, a laparoscopy for endometriosis, two partial hyster-ectomies, an appendectomy, and a surgery to remove scar tissue and a cyst. (One more *partial* and I'll have a complete *royal flush*–literally, all my female parts will be completely flushed!) Yet in the pain I believe God has a purpose for it all, for there to be less of me and more of Him. I confess: when I'm in pain, being kind doesn't come naturally to me. I'm sure if I asked my kids, they'd testify that my heart has a stench when it's impatient or outright rude. Let's be honest. Our flesh is mean and we need God's love to override the natural odor of our flesh which stinketh! I often ask the Lord to help me with my words and thoughts so that God's love will permeate my life.

I pray that today and always you are the sweet fragrance of Christ to those in your life. As you come in contact with people on a daily basis at the bank or the grocery store or even those in your home, may they catch a whiff of God's love as you pass by. When you reveal God's love to them by a kind word or a simple gesture, may it leave God's scent of love and bring a blessing like a fresh bouquet of flowers or a bowl of fresh fruit. May your life permeate every room and place you visit with the fragrance of Christ. When you do, it will be undeniable that God's love has been there and hopefully it will linger there.

Love Suffers Long

Love suffers long.
1 Corinthians 13:4

Chapter 12

"Now for a little while, if need be, you have been grieved by various trials" (1 Peter 1:6). We are living in a day when our joy can easily be robbed by our circumstances if we're not firmly anchored and moored to the foundation of God's Word. Most of us can agree we are either in the thick of a fiery trial or have just gone through a major hardship. Trials won't last forever. Heaven is on the horizon. Jesus is coming soon, so that "little while" in 1 Peter has a greater purpose than we know. 2 Corinthians 4:17 says, "For our light affliction, which is but for a moment, is working for us a far more exceeding and eternal weight of glory."

I have a dear friend who is now with the Lord. She graduated this year and heard the words of her precious Jesus say, "Well done, my good and faithful servant." For years she battled one cancer after another. Knowing her was such a joy. I count it a privilege to have been called her friend. She was like an older sister to me, also becoming "Auntie T" to my kids. It brings tears to my eyes remembering her faith and devotion to Jesus in the midst of her fiery trial.

Knowing her and her heavenly perspective on life she'd be the first to say, "Yes, it was a 'little while,' but look where I am now." Her joy was completely found in her beloved. She loved Psalm 16:11: "Thou wilt shew me the path of life: in Thy presence is fulness of joy; at Thy right hand there are pleasures for evermore." I can imagine her singing the words to this song, "My pain has been set free, and I'm walking hand in hand with the Lord through the Promised Land. So calm your tears and smile, we'll only be apart for a while. 'Cause life . . . is so short, compared to now. I know you're sad, I'll miss you too, but just think what we've got to look forward to. Loved ones know where I've gone." She knew all too well that as a believer God was allowing the pain and suffering in her life for His eternal purposes. She never questioned God with, "Why me?" Her response was always, "Why not me?" It was shared at her memorial service how the last few months before she went to be with the Lord she was reading the book of 1 Peter that deals with suffering. No doubt this verse spoke to her, "To this you were called, because Christ suffered for you, leaving you an example, that you should follow in His steps" (1 Peter 2:21). She will forever be to me a living and dying example of a woman fruitful in affliction.

I remember when Terry and I were at a ladies' retreat years ago. We were together in our room when a friend brought the devotional *Streams in the Desert* to Terry. It was November 6th and she had just been told by the doctor that another breast cancer was found. The verse for that day was Revelation

3:19, "Those whom I love I rebuke and discipline."

> God selects the best and most notable of His servants for the best and most notable afflictions, for those who have received the most grace from Him are able to endure the most afflictions. In fact, an affliction hits a believer never by chance but by God's divine direction. He does not haphazardly aim His arrows, for each one is on a special mission and touches only the heart for whom it is intended. It is not only the grace of God but also His glory that is revealed when a believer can stand and quietly endure an affliction. (Joseph Caryl)

"Now for a little while, if need be, you have been grieved by various trials" (1 Peter 4:15). Those three little words: *if need be* . . . "Really, Lord? Is all this necessary?" we might ask. The answer is yes. "As for God His ways are perfect." Not sometimes perfect or 90% of the time perfect—ALL His ways are perfect. And like the master goldsmith, He's removing the dross from our lives that we might be conformed to the image of His Son. It's been said that it took forty years for the Children of Israel to get out of Egypt, but it took a lifetime to get Egypt out of the Children of Israel.

Like a loving parent who corrects a child to keep them from harm, our heavenly Father will also correct us in love to prevent us from getting run over by our flesh and sin. He must strip us from the worldliness and carnality that creeps in. "My son, do not make light of the Lord's discipline, and do not lose heart when He rebukes you, because the Lord disciplines the one He loves, and He chastens everyone He accepts as His son" (Heb. 12:5-6). As a parent of three children, I have many times had to take them to my office (the downstairs bathroom) and correct them for disobeying, with the purpose of teaching them obedience, right from wrong. "No discipline seems pleasant at the time, but painful. Later on, however, it produces a harvest of righteousness and peace for those who have been trained by it" (Heb. 12:11). Ask any child who's just had the "board of education applied to the seat of learning" if it was enjoyable. Chances are they will say, "No, it hurts." But ask the parent, "Do you enjoy disciplining your child?" And she will say, "No, it hurts me more than it hurts them." So why do we do it? Because we love them and desire to train them up to be well-behaved children and not spoiled brats. That's the first thing that comes to mind. Correction says, "This behavior—unkindness, rudeness, disobedience or hurting another person—is wrong and not acceptable. Behind the heart of the parent is love and goodwill for the child. How much more does our Father love us and desire to prepare us for heaven? He who did not spare His own Son, but willingly allowed Him to purify us from our sins, has a purpose in every trial we face. There's a harvest of love, joy, peace, patience, kindness, goodness, faithfulness, gentleness and self-control that will spring forth from our lives as the Holy Spirit works in and through us by the trials we face.

I've been learning *patience* and what real love is every day I spend with my daughter who has special needs. The Lord is filling me with his patience daily. Patience is defined by Noah Webster in many ways, these are my favorites: "composure without murmuring, calm and constant diligence without agitation and uneasiness; persevering, constant in pursuit, calmly diligent." Ask any mother of a 2-year-old about being patient. It certainly isn't something we can manifest ourselves, but wholly a work of God and His Spirit filling and occupying us with more of himself. Last night in church we sang, "More love, more power, more of You in my life." How we need more of Him, every hour of our day. Jesus said, "A new command I give you: Love one another. . . . By this all men will know that you are My disciples, if you love one another" (John 13:34-35).

How do I show my daughter love? By being patient with her when she struggles to put a sentence together. I love her when I take the time to listen as she tries to express herself. I love her by not exploding when she's made a complete disaster of her room and says, "I never do that again." It's not always easy, but the Lord is able to give us composure under pressure and a calm diligence without agitation. Jesus is our Great High Priest who sympathizes with our weaknesses. He was in all points tempted as we are, yet without sin (Heb. 4:15). Jesus knows what we face; he's been there, through more than we'll ever know this side of heaven. He understands and sees our hearts. He is ready and willing to fill us with His patient love.

Synonyms for *patience* are unwavering, unfaltering, unflinching, without fail, through thick and thin, sink or swim, rain or shine, steadiness, steadfast, resolve, will, clear grit and strength of mind. *Patience* speaks of perseverance, continuance, to persist, hold on, hold out, stick to, carry on, keep on, and cling to. This reminds me of my precious friend Terry who preserved in her fiery trial with cancer. She was steadfast, immovable, always abounding in the Lord. Her faith and love for the Lord was unwavering, unfaltering, unflinching. She loved the Lord with true grit, and regardless of the pain she praised her Beloved Jesus. Her love for Him suffered long and patiently, endured ever so quietly.

1 Corinthians 13:4 says, "Love is patient." God's *agape* love is certainly unwavering; it falters not, and is the perfect example of unflinching, without fail. Think of Jesus on the cross. It's been said that it wasn't the nails that held Him there, but His love for you and me. While pinned to the tree, He never flinched and did not waver for one second. He patiently endured the cross, the pain, and the shame knowing it would purchase our pardon and set us free. He suffered in our place. "Beloved, do not think it strange concerning the fiery trial which is to try you, as though some strange thing happened to you; but rejoice to the extent that you partake of Christ's sufferings, that when His glory is revealed, you may also be glad with exceeding joy" (1 Peter 4:12-13).

For myself, being a parent of a child with special needs, I am still learning to love with patience. In my flesh my love wavers, falters and fails miserably. But gratefully, the Lord's love never runs out. During those years when Grace Ann was silent (about 6-7 of them in total), it was extremely painful to walk through. I remember her first day of kindergarten in the special ed class. Would her teacher understand her needs? How would Grace Ann be able to communicate when she needed help? Would she be okay? Sometimes the Lord calls us to suffer long in a trial. The last nine years have been a silent sorrow. I've kept the pain to myself for the most part, only sharing with a few close friends my heartache and prayer requests. The good news is that the suffering is not in vain. The outcome is fruitful if we choose to keep the Lord as our focus. This is a verse I've always fallen back on and it has sustained me: "And let us not grow weary while doing good, for in due season we shall reap if we do not lose heart" (Gal. 6:9).

"God is faithful, who will not allow you to be tempted beyond what you are able" (1 Cor. 10:13). "And now abide faith, hope, love, these three; but the greatest of these is love" (1 Cor. 13:13). When you are in need of love, look to Jesus. He is unlimited in His supply. May the grace and glory of God be revealed in your life as you "stand and quietly endure" the affliction you are in—praying, "Make me fruitful in this for your glory, Lord."

Love Is Kind

But when the kindness and love of God our Savior appeared, He saved us, not because of righteous things we had done, but because of his mercy.
Titus 3:4-5

Chapter 13

"But the fruit of the Spirit is love, joy, peace, patience, kindness . . ." (Gal. 5:22). Jesus is the embodiment of true kindness. His love for us has been revealed through His kindness shown throughout the Word of God. This is how I spell kindness:

K—Care & concern. The kindness of God cares for others; it is concerned for people's welfare. (Care and concern don't start with a *K* but you know where I'm going.) 1 Peter 5:7 says, "Casting all your care upon Him, for He cares for you." When the 5,000 were hungry, Jesus cared about their lives practically. He had compassion on them because they were like sheep without a shepherd (Mark 6:34). It was getting late in the afternoon (Luke 9:12) and out of his kindness and love Jesus provided lunch for everyone with plenty of leftovers.

I—Invests. The kindness of God invests time and effort into people's lives, showing a genuine interest in them. "Let each of you look out not only for your own interests, but also for the interests of others" (Phil. 2:4). One of the synagogue rulers, Jairus, came to Jesus because his daughter was dying. Jesus took an interest in the life of a little girl and the faith of a desperate father. Ultimately Jesus healed Jairus' daughter (Mark 5:22-43).

N—Never-ending. The kindness of God is never-ending. "For the mountains shall depart and the hills be removed, but My kindness shall not depart from you" (Isaiah 54:10).

D—Demonstration. The kindness of God demonstrates itself in action which results in love, benefiting all mankind. "But God demonstrates His own love toward us, in that while we were still sinners, Christ died for us" (Rom. 5:8).

N—Notices others. The kindness of God notices the needs of people. "When Jesus came into Peter's house, He saw Peter's mother-in-law lying in bed with a fever. He touched her hand and the fever left her, and she got up and began to wait on him" (Matt. 8:14-15).

E—Eternally-minded. The kindness of God is eternally-minded. "But You are a God ready to pardon, gracious and merciful, slow to anger, abundant in kindness" (Nehemiah 9:17). God is eternal and it is in His nature to be abundantly kind.

S—Speaks. The kindness of God speaks a blessing. Speaking of Jesus, "So all bore witness to Him, and marveled at the gracious words which proceeded out of His mouth" (Luke 4:22). Our example is always Jesus, but also the Proverbs 31 woman: "She opens her mouth with wisdom, and on her tongue is the law of kindness" (Prov. 31:26).

S—Serves others. The kindness of God serves people unconditionally. "But love your enemies, do good, and lend, hoping for nothing in return; and your reward will be great, and you will be sons of the Most High. For He is kind to the unthankful and evil" (Luke 6:35).

Great is the mystery of godliness: "God was manifested in the flesh" (1 Tim. 3:16). We get our English word manifest from the Latin word manifestus which means "plain, clear, to make smooth, to explain, clearness, openness, expanding, extending, clearly visible to the eye or obvious to the understanding; apparent, not obscure or difficult to be seen or understood; to reveal, to make public, to display."

The kindest act in all of history was when God the Father and His Son determined that salvation would come to mankind in the clearest way possible, the manifestation of God incarnate. For years He foretold of His Son's coming in His Word, so that the Messiah wouldn't be missed. His prophets explained the details of His Son's arrival with such exactness that when you present the truth to children they understand it. The Gospel couldn't be clearer. "For God so loved the world that He gave His only begotten Son, that whoever believes in Him should not perish but have everlasting life" (John 3:16). It's the love of God that compelled Him to send His Son on the greatest mission ever: to redeem mankind. "I have loved you with an everlasting love" (Jer. 31:3).

The Father was "not willing that any should perish but that all should come to repentance" (2 Peter 3:9).

Heaven concealed the glory of God and His Son's love until one night when God himself came out of obscurity and dwelt among us openly. "When the fullness of the time had come, God sent forth His Son, born of a woman, born under the law, to redeem those who were under the law, that we might receive the adoption as sons" (Gal. 4:4-5). The Lord made His kindness "plain and clearly visible to the eyes of man." There were those 2,000 years ago who, with their own eyes, saw the face of God when they beheld Jesus. Their hands touched him. Hundreds were healed and touched by him. Their ears heard the voice of God when He spoke. For many who had received His touch, His love, His forgiveness and kindness, it couldn't have been more apparent or obvious who they had witnessed. For Jesus displayed his kindness like no other man in all of History. He loved people to death. His love was publicly made known for the entire world to see when He died with outstretched arms upon the cross. God himself chose to suffer the most horrific, bloody and violent death imaginable so that there would never be a doubt as to His loving kindness.

Why would the Creator reduce himself to something so small, so dependent and so utterly incapable like an infant? Perhaps He thought it was the best way to wrap His gift. Just like Christmas presents wrapped and ready to be opened on Christmas morning. "The Word became flesh and made his dwelling among us. We have seen His glory, the glory of the One and Only, who came from the Father, full of grace and truth" (John 1:14). I love wrapping gifts for my kids at Christmas time. I love watching the wonder in their eyes as they come downstairs on Christmas morning in anticipation of opening their gifts. The Christmas tree is decorated and the presents are all wrapped and labeled with names on them just waiting to be opened. It's all before their eyes in plain view. God sent his Son wrapped in perfect softness and holy innocence, because He knew it would be the clearest way for man to know his kindness. Years later, the baby in the manger would grow up. And as Messiah, He willingly laid down his life. "And being found in appearance as a man, He humbled himself and became obedient to death, even death on a cross" (Phil. 2:8). After being scourged and nailed to the cross His first words were, "Father, forgive them, for they do not know what they do" (Luke 23:34). Manifesting such kindness the world has never known. His last cry would be, "It is finished" (John 19:30), declaring His mission accomplished. "For the Son of Man has come to seek and to save that which was lost" (Luke 19:10).

Jesus left us an example to follow: "Be kind and compassionate to one another, forgiving each other, just as in Christ God forgave you" (Eph. 4:32). What does it mean to be kind? Kindness is "disposed to do good to others; having tenderness or goodness of nature." Ask the Lord to display His kindness through your life to those around you. When you have the opportunity, show your husband, your family and your friends that you care about them by speaking a kind word. Remember the fruit of the Spirit is love. Love is demonstrated in kindness extended to others. Kindness lets the other person have the right of way in the parking lot. Kindness asks how she is doing and listens to her response. Kindness waters a plant when it's not even your own. My dear neighbor Mike has been watering my front porch plant for me. (I told you I don't have a green thumb.) No wonder it looks so good and is blooming so much lately. He is so kind. Even in pain he is thoughtful! Kindness gives and serves to bless others. Kindness forgives when it's been hurt. May you continually be filled with His kindness. "Therefore, as God's chosen people, holy and dearly loved, clothe yourselves with compassion, kindness, humility, gentleness and patience" (Col. 3:12).

Love Is Not Rude

Love . . . is not boastful or vainglorious,
does not display itself haughtily. It is not conceited
(arrogant and inflated with pride); it is not rude
(unmannerly) and does not act unbecomingly.
1 Corinthians 13:4-5

Chapter 14

Peter had the incredible privilege of witnessing firsthand the love of our Savior throughout the three years that he was His disciple. "We did not follow cunningly devised fables when we made known to you the power and coming of our Lord Jesus Christ, but were eyewitnesses of His majesty" (2 Peter 1:16). He most likely observed Jesus as He talked with a woman who was an outcast of society and offered her living water that she might never thirst again (John 4). Jesus didn't ignore her. This wasn't something that was done in their day. It was not acceptable for a Jew to talk with a Samaritan. Yet the love of God knows no racial limits. Jesus purposely sought out a woman who was literally searching for love in all the wrong places. He wasn't rude, but remarkably loving. Peter was there when Jesus healed the paralytic not only of his disease but of his sins. The scribes thought His actions were blasphemous. Yet Jesus in His love and compassion forgave and healed the man (Matt. 9). The list goes on of individuals that Jesus loved and ministered to. He was never rude, self-seeking or out of time for people. Peter eye-witnessed firsthand the love of God in action on a practical level as well as a spiritual level. Oh, that we would learn from the example of Jesus' love, to love in word and deed as He did. It isn't impossible for He has given us His Holy Spirit who will love through us, touching those around us.

"Love is not proud." *Proud* is "arrogant, haughty, possessing a high or unreasonable conceit of one's own excellence." We've all met someone at one time or another who was proud and arrogant. It's tragic that the cults of the day that preach salvation by works (a false doctrine) breed arrogance and a conceit about their works. God specifically chose the foolish things of this world, as well as the weak and the despised, to shame the wise . . . so that NO ONE may boast before Him (1 Cor. 1:27, 29). Jesus, who had every right to proclaim his majesty and declare His glory, chose to be humble and meek. He never acted in a haughty manner. God's love condescended. Jesus humbled himself and made himself of no reputation. He became obedient to death, even the death of the cross (Phil. 2:7-8). We are told that God opposes the proud but gives grace to the humble (1 Pet. 5:5). And in Proverbs 16:5 it says, "The Lord detests all the proud of heart." With all the greatness that Jesus possessed as God Incarnate, He never boasted in His accomplishments. He simply loved the hurting, the sick, the blind, the lame and the lost souls of His day. He honored His Father and came to fulfill His will.

May we walk in lowliness of mind and follow the pattern of our beloved Jesus. When we realize who we are in light of who God is we discover there is nothing to be proud of in our flesh. There is no good thing within us (Rom. 7:18). Thankfully, as new creatures in Christ, we've been given a new nature. May the Lord's love touch those around us as His Spirit equips us.

Love is not rude. Rude behavior is something as a parent I do not tolerate with my kids. My desire is to teach them to behave in a loving manner. *Rude* is "rough, course manners, uncivil, and harsh." Synonyms for *rude* are "bad manners, disrespect, ill temper, insult, give a cold shoulder to; to keep at a distance; impolite, ungracious, bitter, crusty, sour and sharp." These words paint an unpleasant portrait of rude behavior which is something totally contrary to the love of God. I'm continually teaching my kids to speak with manners and be polite. It seems to be a constant challenge in a society that doesn't value respect. When something is said that comes out rude, I quickly remind them to correct it and I pray the law of kindness stays on their lips. Manners matter. And character counts. As women of God we have the plumb line of God's Word to measure our behavior when we fall short. What a joy that we have the Holy Spirit to rely on in this process of fruitful living.

We are told in Ephesians 5:2, "Walk in love, as Christ also has loved us and given himself for us, an offering and a sacrifice to God for a sweet-smelling aroma." Think of Jesus being taken to be scourged. If you've seen *The Passion of the Christ* you know how horrible the flogging of Jesus was. The unimaginable loss of blood He endured. Isaiah 53:3-9 recalls the suffering Savior and the sacrifice of His love. Here are just a few excerpts: "He is despised and rejected by men, a Man of sorrows and acquainted with grief. . . . He was wounded for our transgressions . . . He was oppressed and He was afflicted, yet He opened not His mouth; He was led as a lamb to the slaughter, and as a sheep before it's shearers is silent, so He opened not His mouth. . . . He had done no violence, nor was any deceit in His mouth."

Our precious Jesus, the Lamb of God who takes away the sins of the world, opened not His mouth, not a word. In the midst of being beaten and scourged, He loved. We will never be able to comprehend the vast amount of pain He endured or the loss of blood suffered. It certainly was unimaginable; some men died during a Roman scourging due to the loss of blood and organ failure. We will never suffer on the same level of Jesus. Have you ever hurt yourself accidently cooking or stubbed your toe on the corner of a coffee table? What came out? Were you silent like Jesus? Or was it something rude? A little stubbed toe hardly compares to what Jesus endured, but it shows how rude our sin nature is at the slightest pain or injury.

"And when they had come to the place called Calvary, there they crucified Him. . . . Then Jesus said, 'Father, forgive them, for they do not know what they do'" (Luke 23:33-34). Jesus' very first words after being nailed to the cross were words of love and forgiveness, nothing rude or ill-mannered. Prior to this in Matthew 27:30-31, "They spit on Him, and took the staff and struck Him on the head again and again. After they had mocked Him, they took off the robe and put His own clothes on Him." Not once do we see Jesus ungracious, short-tempered or bitter; it's simply not in His nature. The Love of Jesus is continually courteous, perfectly polite, gracious and gentle. What better picture is there of God's love in action than the cross?

Our love falls so short of Christ's. How many times in a day are we quick to speak a sharp word to our kids or husbands? We are so inclined in our flesh to be bad-tempered and ungracious rather than loving and kind. I remember at my wedding my pastor telling my husband and me that our love would run out for each other. "God has poured out His love into our hearts by the Holy Spirit, whom He has given us" (Rom. 5:5). I'm so thankful that the Spirit is there to take over in our weakness. His love never runs out. Ask Him for His love to fill you and to permeate your life. Perhaps in those moments of pain, something of Him will be seen or come out instead of something sinful and rude.

"Little children, let us not love [merely] in theory or in speech but in deed and in truth (in practice and in sincerity)" (1 John 3:18). We love with our actions. Love is a verb not a feeling. I truly love my husband or children when I respond to them gently, graciously, politely, not rudely. Oh, that we would come to the Lord for His love to be shed abroad in our hearts. Then and only then will we walk in His love.

In Galatians 6:14 Paul said, "May I never boast except in the cross of our Lord Jesus Christ, through which the world has been crucified to me, and I to the world." Thankfully, "it is by grace you have been saved, through faith—and this not from yourselves, it is the gift of God—not by works, so that no one can boast" (Eph. 2:8-9). May you celebrate the Lord's love and boast only in Him!

Love Is Not Self-Seeking

Love . . . is not self-seeking.
1 Corinthians 13:5

Chapter 15

"Love (God's love in us) does not insist on its own rights or its own way, for it is not self-seeking" (1 Cor. 13:5). In our society today, everything seems to be centered on *self* and *my rights*. That mindset is so contrary to the heart of God. Jesus' love is others-centered. The Lord loved the world and it stirred His heart to have compassion on souls that needed to be saved. He chose to die and accept the pain that the cross would bring to him (John 3:16). "As the time approached for him to be taken up to heaven, Jesus resolutely set out for Jerusalem" (Luke 9:51). He fixed His heart on His mission and didn't deter from it. Jesus said, "Greater love has no one than this, than to lay down one's life for his friends" (John 15:13). He didn't hold on to His rights as King God. Since He is our example of how to love, we learn from Him that love is selfless and surrenders voluntarily.

We live in an extremely self-centered world. Most people go about living their lives with only one thought: me. As we continue to learn and desire to be fruitful, we know that fruit comes from a life filled with the Spirit of God. Apart from Him there is no good thing within us, which is clearly seen by the acts of our flesh. "The acts of the sinful nature are obvious: . . . idolatry and witchcraft; hatred, discord, jealousy, fits of rage, selfish ambition, dissensions, factions" (Gal. 5:19-20). I find it interesting that selfish ambition is lumped in with witchcraft, which is as the sin of rebellion (1 Sam. 15:23). Can it really be that bad? Let's find out what the Word of God has to say about selfishness.

Selfishness is "that supreme self-love or self-preference which leads a person in his actions to direct his purposes to the advancement of his own happiness without regarding the interest of others." The world's philosophy is "every man for himself." We are told in Philippians 2:3-5, "Do nothing out of selfish ambition or vain conceit, but in humility consider others better than yourselves. Each of you should look not only to your own interests, but also to the interests of others. Your attitude should be the same as that of Christ Jesus." What was the attitude of Jesus? Humble, serving others, obedient to death, loving!

Love is not self-seeking because it doesn't even consider self. This is a totally foreign concept for our flesh which is constantly seeking to be pampered, fed and nurtured. As we mature in the Lord, hopefully we are moving from being self-indulgent and living for ourselves to living for God and others and denying self. Honestly, our sinful nature loves itself too much. It wants meals promptly and snacks too. And if it doesn't get fed on time, it lets you know by a nasty growl from below that screams, "Feed Me." What about sleep? (Speaking as a person who desperately needs her sleep.) When you have a newborn baby that needs to eat every three hours, you quickly learn to lay aside your *right* to sleep through the night. Mothers learn right away to put the interests of their baby before their own needs and wants, even when it comes to precious sleep.

Synonyms for *selfish* are egotistic, someone who thinks highly of herself and is consumed with self, self-indulgent and self-worshipping. They are narrow-minded, unspiritual and earthly-minded as well. What an accurate picture of our flesh, focusing solely on itself. The antonyms of *selfish* are virtue, excellence, right-minded, whole-souled, godlike! Doesn't it make sense that because of the Fall our souls are not whole until Jesus comes into our hearts and takes up residence within our lives? Then and only then are we whole-souled. As He fills us with His Spirit each day, may we pattern our lives after our precious Jesus, following His example to love others first and not insist on our own way!

Love Is Not Easily Angered

Love . . . is not easily angered.
I Corinthians 13:5

Chapter 16

"The Lord is gracious and compassionate; slow to anger and rich in love" (Psalm 145:8). I'm so thankful that God is slow to anger. He's not impulsive or explosive like we tend to be. He takes His time with people with limitless mercy. The Children of Israel disobeyed year after year and the Lord always exercised mercy as He dealt with them. It was Moses' moment of anger when he smote the rock twice to bring forth water that kept him from entering the Promised Land. He misrepresented God to the people. Jesus was the rock, who was only smitten once on the cross. We see over and over again, "Their hearts were not loyal to Him, they were not faithful to His covenant. Yet He was merciful; He forgave their iniquities and did not destroy them. Time after time He restrained His anger and did not stir up His full wrath" (Psalm 78:37-38). The Lord even showed grace to Moses by bringing him in to the Promised Land years later when he appeared on the Mount of Transformation with Jesus (Matt. 17:1-6).

We are told in Ephesians 4:26, "'In your anger do not sin': Do not let the sun go down while you are

78

still angry." It's not that love doesn't get angry at all, but it doesn't boil over and sin. Jesus was angered over the religious leaders who had turned His House of Prayer into a den of thieves. Yet He did not sin. Those men who were supposed to be representing God to the people were robbing the people with fees for temple sacrifices and actually making it more difficult for the people to worship God. Each one of us is a work in progress. You may have more patience than I do when it comes to what makes you angry. This is one area I'm sure we can all grow in. James says it best, "My dear brothers, take note of this: Everyone should be quick to listen, slow to speak and slow to become angry, for man's anger does not bring about the righteous life that God desires" (James 1:19-20). This is what we are after: a fruitful life pleasing God, and His righteousness abounding in our lives. We will get angry, but Lord willing it won't boil over and lead to sin.

The Lord is continually teaching me, especially with my kids, to talk first and not go into an angry mode right away. When I see Legos all over the bed and floor, I so need the Lord to fill me with His love so that I do not respond hastily as I want the mess cleaned up ASAP! (Amazingly, it's not a mess to my twelve-year-old; it's me that has the problem.) The Lord is working in my heart daily, helping me not be so easily angered. It really is the little things that get to us, isn't it? A simple misunderstanding has the potential of being blown out of proportion like someone dumping out the coffee when we were going to drink it. "A gentle answer turns away wrath, but a harsh word stirs up anger" (Prov. 15:1). I've learned over the years that speaking quietly keeps the peace. This is an ongoing work believe me! It's amazing how one loud voice can put you on the defensive, and then your tendency is to respond loudly too. When voices get louder on both sides emotions tend to soar and the problem is only worsened. May the Lord help us to be slow to anger and to lengthen our fuse. Slow simply means "not hasty, acting with deliberation."

Amy Carmichael prayed, "Thy sweetness, Lord," as an arrow prayer when she needed deliverance from a situation quickly. In opposition to whatever came her way, she prayed the opposite of the attack, going on the offensive (*Edges of His Ways*, pg. 100). They say, "The best defense is a good offense." We too can pray, "Your love, Lord; Your patience, Lord." My favorite is "help, please!" It's not long or complicated. The Lord knows our hearts and sees our challenges, especially when it comes to dealing with children. Sometimes they can bring out the worst in us, which makes the grace of God all the more wonderful. He is not easily angered with us but, oh, so patient and loving! This is why we need to be in constant communication with the Lord, praying throughout the day. If being easily angered is something you're struggling with, ask the Lord for His help. He will do exceedingly, abundantly above all you could ask or think, and fill you with His *agape* love.

As I ponder "love is not easily angered," it really comes down to, "What are we filled with?" If I'm filled with the Lord and His love, then those little things that tend to get me quite easily angered won't bother me so much. One morning I came downstairs to a messy kitchen, which I really dislike (to put it mildly). Dirty dishes were still in the sink from the night before, the toaster was left out and the dishwasher hadn't been started. In my flesh, I could have easily been angry that the mess wasn't cleaned up by the child who was told to take care of it. (Just so you know this child is a teenager who is capable of the responsibility!) In that moment, the Lord brought me a victory, as He reminded me to be "slow to anger" and to pray, "Thy sweetness, Lord," in exchange for my frustration and irritation. He is so ready to impart His loving patience when we ask for it. I was then able to talk to my teenager with the Lord's gentleness about following through with the chores—in love and not in anger. Yeah, God! It is my prayer that there would be more of Jesus and less of me. May He increase and we decrease. Before you get out of bed in the morning, come to His throne of grace for a fresh filling of His love which knows no limits. He will refill you and cause your cup to overflow!

Love Keeps No Record of Wrongs

Love . . . keeps no record of wrongs.
1 Corinthians 13:5

Chapter 17

Love "takes no account of the evil done to it (it pays no attention to a suffered wrong)." I love the Amplified Version of the Bible because it always paints such a vivid picture in my mind of God's Word. I think back to Joseph who was betrayed by his brothers, falsely accused by Potifer's wife and thrown in prison unjustly. In the end he forgives his brothers, keeping no record of the wrong things they had done to him. Joseph becomes a type of Christ for us, revealing the heart of our Savior, who did not pay attention to the things He suffered but willingly chose to love instead.

Such love is hard to grasp. Do we know anything of God's love that keeps no account when we are hurt or wronged? Or are we keeping a book and checking it twice each time something comes our way that offends us? We will never be able to fully grasp the evil onslaught of the enemy that was unleashed upon our Lord by the gates of hell. Watching *The Chronicles of Narnia*, I couldn't help but think of Jesus. When Aslan was brought to the stone table with all those horrible, wretched beasts hurling insults and mocking Him, my heart thought about Jesus as He carried His cross up to Calvary and was crucified there. Yes, there was the crowd before Him, mocking Him, taunting Him to come down from the cross, "'You who are going to destroy the temple and build it in three days, save Yourself! Come down from the cross, if You are the Son of God!' In the same way the chief priests, the teachers of the law and the elders mocked Him. 'He saved others,' they said, 'but He can't save himself! He's the King of Israel! Let Him come down now from the cross, and we will believe in Him'" (Matt. 27:40-42). Was that crowd inspired by hell itself to deter Jesus from His one mission to save mankind?

Throughout Jesus' ministry the enemy continually tried to keep Him from the cross. Yet God's love was stronger than the demons of hell, stronger than any sin, stronger than any insult that was hurled His way. The very first cry of Jesus from the cross was, "Father, forgive them, for they know not what they do" (Luke 23:34). Oh, that we might be filled with that kind of love that keeps no record of wrongs done unto us.

There is no exhausting the supply of God's love. Psalm 145:8 says that not only is God "slow to anger," but He is "rich in love." There are countless wrongs which come our way in this fallen world. Some I can't begin to understand, like murder or rape. But the God we know and love has limitless resources to cover all sin and the wrongs that have been done to us. God's *agape* love is never insufficient, inadequate or deficient. His love never ebbs and flows like our love can. His supply never runs dry. There is no draining or deleting it. His love is never under the threat of running scarce. And amazing as it is, God is never stingy with His love like we can be. He doesn't ever hold back His love, even for the worst of offenses. When Jesus died, His blood was shed for ALL mankind, to atone for ALL sin and for every wrong. God doesn't pick and choose those who can be forgiven and those who cannot be forgiven. *All* means ALL. Think of the worst atrocities committed in this world by man, and even that is covered by the precious blood of Jesus and forgiven.

As women, we can quickly have our feelings hurt. Our emotions, being what they are on any given day, can cause us to be more touchy or sensitive to certain things. Misunderstandings and words can be taken the wrong way and can easily be blown out of proportion in our minds. We can replay a conversation over and over and get hung up with bitterness and unforgiveness. May we be quick to take those hurts to the Lord and lay them at His feet. We do not want accounting ledgers in our hearts of offenses and hurts that keep God's love from flowing through us. Not only does God "keep no record of our sin," but He removes it and remembers it no more: "As far as the east is from the west, so far has He removed our transgressions from us" (Psalm 103:12). "For I will forgive their iniquity, and their sin I will remember no more" (Jer. 31:34).

Sometimes we need to have a good case of short-term memory loss! To *forget* means to have "a short memory, out of mind, buried or sank in oblivion, amnesia." The Lord has buried our sins under the blood of Jesus; there is no bringing it back. "If we confess our sins, He is faithful and just to forgive us our sins and to cleanse us from all unrighteousness" (1 John 1:9).

In learning to keep no record of wrongs, we must remember that we too have wronged God and others. Thankfully He has removed our sin and wiped our slate clean. If we desire that same love and forgiveness for ourselves, we must be willing to offer it to others who have perhaps hurt us. We've all suffered hurts. Some are greater than others. If there's a past wrong or hurt that keeps gnawing at you, allow the Lord to heal it and take if off your accounting books. "Their sins and their lawless deeds I will remember no more" (Heb. 10:17). May God's Spirit enable us to keep shorter accounts with others and love them with His love.

Pure Joy

Consider it pure joy, my brothers,
whenever you face trials of many kinds, because
you know that the testing of your faith
develops perseverance.
James 1:2-3

Chapter 18

What's on your top ten list of things that bring you pure joy? Below is my list. Now each one is a joy in and of itself, but I had to start somewhere so, working backwards, here we go!

#10—A friend of mine just had a baby last week. Gazing at this little miracle of life was such a joy! Babies are a pure delight. Their tiny little toes and fingers and sweet, precious faces are just a wonder to behold. Nothing smells as good as a new baby.

#9—If you've had the blessing of having your own children, you know what a joy it is to hear their first words and watch them take their first steps. (It is especially joyful to hear those first words and sentences when they've been silent for years!)

#8—Having breakfast with the ladies from church on Saturday morning at Mimi's Cafe. We share time together in the Word and in fellowship, and we share prayer requests. What a joy.

#7—Reading a really good book! There are so

many to choose from.

#6—Getting together with my good friend Nancy and her kids for some R&R at the pool during the summer. Our kids all play together and have such a great time.

#5—Last summer's mission trip to Hungary with our team from church. What a blessing to serve the kids there at the VBS with friends that are like family. The body of Christ is truly a joy!

#4—Just being at home with my husband and kids. A simple but pure joy.

#3—Being caught up in the heavenlies during worship—anytime, anywhere. It could be driving in traffic or having a quiet worship time alone or Sunday mornings at church.

#2—Sunday mornings are a pure joy for me. I love my church and church family. Being with the family of God, hearing the Word taught by my pastor, having the Spirit of God speak to my heart, gathering with friends—what could be better? Just one thing!

#1—Waking up early and spending time with Jesus at His feet. Having Him all to myself; hearing His sweet voice impart the truth of His Word. Breaking bread with Him and finding the nourishment for my heart and soul. He is my great joy and delight!

Somehow *trials* didn't make my top ten list of pure joys. Could it be that my perspective on trials and God's perspective differ? The Lord sees trials working for my ultimate good: the testing of my faith, developing something called perseverance. When I'm in a trial, I don't always see clearly the end result He has in mind. But I know from the Word that it's working for good to build me up in my most holy faith.

"For the Lord God is a sun and shield; the Lord will give grace and glory; no good thing will He withhold from those who walk uprightly" (Psalm 84:11). I love this promise. It is my life verse and the banner over my head. It reminds me that the Father is there to bless us, protect us and provide for us. The key is what I see as good may be different in God's economy. "No good thing will He withhold from me." That means if the trials I'm in will bring out something of eternal value—like His love or joy, peace or patience, or in this case perseverance—then I must re-evaluate what *good* really is. This verse assures me that no matter what "IT'S ALL GOOD," especially when life hurts and circumstances don't make sense. I always go back to this truth. It's going to be good in the end; I have my Father's promise. He's going to give me grace to see me through. And one day it will all be glorious in heaven bringing my Jesus glory which is my heart's desire.

We've been going through the Book of Acts on Sunday mornings at church. It never ceases to amaze me the trials Paul endured. His example as a man filled with the Spirit and fruitful no matter what came his way challenges me and inspires me to keep pressing on. In Acts 16:16-40 Paul casts a demon out of a slave girl who "earned a great deal of money for her owners." Once she was delivered of the demon, the slave owners were out of a paycheck. The men seized Paul and Silas, made false accusations against them resulting in them being "severely flogged and thrown in prison with their feet fastened." Does this seem like a good thing? Honestly, if I were Paul and writing my *Pure Joy Top Ten* list of things I did over the summer, this would not be one of them. Paul and Silas don't throw a pity party in their darkest hour, but rather praise God and sing worship songs at midnight. What an example for us. You may not feel like singing, but when you choose to praise Him He will do an amazing thing in your heart. I guarantee you, it will be good!

There have been times in my life, when I've been in physical pain and unable to sing out loud. But by God's grace I've been brought into His presence as I listen to a worship CD or my iPod and sing to the Lord in my heart. The other day as I was driving, the song "I Will Praise You in the Storm" by Casting Crowns came on. This song did something to lift my heart and give me hope in the midst of a trying day. It renewed my joy, bringing me to center my thoughts on Jesus during the trial I was facing. And as my perspective was readjusted, the Lord caused my heart to overflow with His Spirit. Worship is the key that sets us free. The enemy wants to keep us down and discouraged, depressed and despondent. But when we choose to turn our eyes upon Jesus and realize that He is the One who takes our hand and walks with us, who leads us and guides us, it's all pure joy from there on. Another great song of encouragement is The Kry's song "Take My Hand and Walk." Keep the worship going in your heart; you will see the prison doors open.

Paul and Silas had an apparent affect on the other

prisoners while they praised the Lord. Suddenly the earth shook with a "violent earthquake" and the prison doors were opened. In the end, the jailer and his household were saved. Their lives were touched by the Spirit of God as Paul and Silas worshipped God in the midst of the jail.

Let me ask you a hard question: When Jesus is ALL you have can you say, "He is enough?" Can you just rest in His presence and praise Him for who He is regardless of where you are? We have a choice to make: to panic in our flesh or praise Him in our Spirit. Do you know that you know that God will take care of you? When do we find God faithful? When we desperately need Him to be! It's not until I'm in a fix and cry out to Him for deliverance that I see His faithfulness and ability to come through for me. Where did Paul write this valuable letter? In a prison. I've visited the Mamertine Prison in Rome where it is believed that Paul was held. It was a dark, dirty hole in the ground. There was no inside light, only that which came from an opening above. Paul went on to pen the Book of Philippians which carries the theme of joy in spite of his suffering. May we, this very day, follow the example of Paul and Silas by praising God no matter what comes our way. And may we too count it a pure joy knowing God is at work in us.

To God, My Joy and My Delight

To God, my joy and my delight.
Psalm 43:4

Chapter 19

Recently we had dear friends of ours visit here in California, taking a furlough from the ministry they are called to in Hungary. I just received an email of selected pictures from their trip. They had many stops along their way, staying with friends, going to the beach, the mountains and even a trip to the Grand Canyon. The Lord truly blessed them with so many great memories. As we travel on in our journey through the fruit of the Spirit, we must take the time to take our snapshots along the way too. Oh, there are so many scenic spots to stop and rest and bask in our Lord's beauty. His love, joy, peace, patience, kindness, goodness and self-control are each a portrait of His character that we desire for ourselves. We don't want to forget for a minute who He is and what He has done for us. Hopefully those pictures will serve as a reminder of what the Lord desires to do in us as well, making us fruitful in every good work.

Our Lord has lavished us with His love and grace in such an amazing way. Salvation belongs to the Lord (Rev. 7:10). It's His to give to any and all who will receive it. What have we been saved from? So many things: the wrath of God, eternal separation from our heavenly Father, the judgment of our sin which Christ absorbed on the cross for us. We're saved from the darkness that so many are in presently. We've been saved to enjoy our Lord for all of eternity which begins here and now. There will be a day when we are reunited with Him in perfect harmony and holiness. In heaven there will be no more pain, no death, no sorrow, no fear, no condemnation and no more sin. To that I say, "Hallelujah!" I hope that you are able to rejoice with me that your reservation has been made by God himself who writes the names of those saved in His Book of Life. "Rejoice because your names are written in heaven" (Luke 10:20).

It was Paul who wrote in 1 Thessalonians 5:16, "Be joyful always" (NIV)—and "Rejoice" (NKJ). Our joy is found solely in Jesus. Joy is independent of our present circumstances and trials. But even in these places the Lord desires to be our joy and bring us to a place where we can look to Him over the hurts we face. There is a stark difference between joy and happiness. I'm happy when life is going good, but we all know this world is not perfect and life gets complicated along the way. We call this life a *pursuit of happiness* because it's like a carrot dangled before us. Perfect happiness is not attainable in this fallen world, but we can possess a genuine joy that this world cannot touch. "Though the fig tree may not blossom, nor fruit be on the vines; though the labor of the olive may fail, and the fields yield no food;

though the flock may be cut off from the fold, and there be no herd in the stalls, yet I will rejoice in the Lord, I will joy in the God of my salvation" (Hab. 3:17-18).

You see, the victory has already been won at the cross. Game over. Although the enemy is a defeated foe, he is not content with losing so he seeks to bring us down however he can. The enemy can never take our salvation away from us. His main ploy is to get us to travel down the road of despair in our thoughts. He whispers his lies, "The end is near, the sky is falling; all hope is gone." He's such a downer because that's the only place he can go, down to the pit. The battle is no longer for our soul but for our mind. If he can get us to that place of focusing on our problems rather than focusing on the Lord, he's succeeded in robbing us of our joy. That's his goal: to rob, kill and destroy (John 10:10). "Yet in all things we are more than conquerors though Him who loved us." Paul went on to say, "For I am persuaded that neither death nor life, nor angels nor principalities nor powers, nor things present nor things to come, nor height nor depth, nor any created thing, shall be able to separate us from the love of God which is in Christ Jesus our Lord" (Rom. 8:38-39).

Do you know this? Are you persuaded by the truth of God's Word and promise to you? It may be that the attacks keep coming. The *what ifs* of the enemy can be relentless. What if my husband doesn't get that raise? What if the car breaks down again? What if this illness never gets better? Silence the *what ifs* with the antidote *who is*. Who is your God? He is strong and mighty to save. "Who is this King of Glory? The Lord strong and mighty" (Ps. 24:8)! "The Lord your God in your midst, the Mighty One, will save; He will rejoice over you with gladness, He will quiet you with His love, He will rejoice over you with singing" (Zeph. 3:17). I love that Jesus is my mighty warrior. He is our perfect defense from the enemy. *Mighty* is "having great bodily strength or physical power, as a mighty arm." Jesus saved us with His outstretched arm on the cross. He was mighty to save then as He withstood the forces of hell, bearing the weight of sin for mankind. *Mighty* also means "valiant, great, wonderful, performed with power." He is mighty to save us now, from any circumstance. There is nothing too hard for the Lord!

Life is so short; it is only but a vapor. All the trials and tribulations will one day fade away and God's eternal joy will be our daily portion. May it be so even now in the midst of the fears that the enemy tries to sneak into our minds. May God's joy so fill our hearts that we keep our perspective on things above. Take the time each day to ponder His goodness. Praise Him for what He has saved you from and what He has saved you to! Thank Him for His gift of grace which is able to bring joy to your heart like nothing else here on earth. Fix your mind on Jesus and all that is wonderful regarding His nature and character. Ask the Lord to give you a proper perspective of your trials in light of eternity. The Lord allows trials to accomplish His purposes in us. He uses them to strengthen our faith, giving us compassion for others, all the while increasing our prayer life. Don't get bogged down by the *what ifs*, remember *who He is*!

Recently the Lord taught me this very lesson. I was concerned about something and how it was all going to work out. The *what ifs* were swirling around in my mind. The Lord reminded me to focus on *who* by rearranging the letters of the word *how*. So often I get bogged down with all that is around me: my pain, the bills, Grace Ann's future. But the Lord spoke to my heart. If I will fix my mind on WHO He is, not the *how*, eventually He will take care of the *how*—He is able to part the Red Sea. "If God is for us, who can be against us?" (Rom. 8:31).

Rejoice in Him—He is your God, your joy and delight!

Intro to Reasons to Rejoice

The joy of the Lord is your strength.
Nehemiah 8:10

Chapter 20

Have you ever been given news that knocked the wind right out of you? Maybe it was a doctor with a certain diagnosis or a spouse with divorce papers. You are left with a horrible, painful feeling in the pit of your stomach, and then the tears of grief just come uncontrollably. You know God's promises in your head, but in that place the emotions just seem so overwhelming and the heartache is so searing that all you can do is cry out to the Lord.

"Where is joy when we can't feel it?" There are those times when we just don't *feel* joyful but we can certainly have God's joy in the midst of it. That's where joy and happiness part company. A friend defined it this way: Happiness has limits and joy is limitless. We still grieve over the death of a parent or child or severe loss. The key is to keep our eyes fixed on Jesus and Offer Yourself to Him—that's choosing JOY. It's not a feeling but an action we take. "Looking unto Jesus" (Heb. 12:2), "Offer Your bodies as living sacrifices, holy and pleasing to God—this is your spiritual act of worship" (Romans 12:1).

Some of you are in survival mode; life has been

one trial after another. Setback after setback and yet in this very place, with emotions raw and wounds still open, I believe God desires to give us His joy to be our strength. It's really the only way we'll make it through the day. Recently, I had a gaping wound that needed to be healed. The Lord was so faithful to tend to it. He is forever our God of all comfort who comforts us so that we can comfort others (2 Cor. 1:4).

Fruit grows over time. It starts as a seed, and as it abides in the branch there is growth. The same is true for us. We don't have to strive or do it on our own. We simply abide in Him, and He in us (John 15) and the fruit will come.

Driving home from church last night, my daughter and I were going through a residential area where some homes already had their Christmas lights up. My daughter was in complete awe. "Oh, look at that one: red, yellow, green, blue lights. Oh, I like that one: snowmen, reindeer and choo choo train. Oh, go that way. Wow, pretty white ones." For a child with speech issues, she had much to say. She was so caught up with the beauty and majesty of the lights; it truly took her breath away. Seeing Christmas lights through the eyes of a child can be so educational. It's interesting that society is compelled to put up lights for several weeks before Christmas—during the darkest time of the year, no more daylight savings. Maybe tradition has said this is how we celebrate, so we all do it. Could it be that within man there is a longing for, a craving after, the Light of the World— Jesus Christ? It's in the darkness that the lights are so beautiful. What if in those dark times we looked to the Light of the World to shine His light in our hearts? And perhaps as we gazed at Him we'd be filled with awe and wonder like my daughter. Oh, did you see that? His limitless love. Oh, look, His matchless mercy. Oh, wow, His glorious grace. And as we turn our eyes upon Jesus looking full at His wonderful face, the things of this world will grow strangely dim in *the light* of his glory and grace!

Here are some reasons to rejoice from Psalm 71. Remember, it's a choice we make.

1. God is our *refuge*—v. 1
2. He is able to *rescue* me—v. 2
3. He is my *rock*—v. 3
4. He is utterly *reliable*—v. 6
5. His *righteousness*—v. 19
6. He *restores* my life again—v. 20
7. He will *revive* me again—v. 20
8. I've been *redeemed*—v. 23

May each one be like a beautiful light that brings you more in awe of who our Savior is and may you be filled with His joy. We have God's promises: "Those who sow in tears will reap with songs of joy" (Ps. 126:5) and "Weeping may endure for a night, but joy comes in the morning" (Psalm 30:5).

Reasons to Rejoice, Part 1: Refuge

In you, O Lord, I have taken refuge.
Psalm 71:1

Chapter 21

In Psalm 71 we have eight *reasons to rejoice*. Eight is the number of *new beginnings*. I pray, if you find yourself in a valley, you see God is the God of the valleys too, and He's able to make you rejoice even there and lift you to the mountaintop.

Our first *R* is *refuge*. Psalm 71:1 says, "In you, O Lord, I have taken refuge." *Refuge* is a shelter or protection from danger or distress. Hebrews 6:18 says, "We have strong consolation, who have fled for refuge to lay hold of the hope set before us." *Refuge* is "that which shelters or protects from calamity, a stronghold which protects by its strength or a sanctuary which secures safety by its sacredness, any place inaccessible to an enemy." "The Lord is a refuge for the oppressed, a stronghold in times of trouble" (Ps. 9:9). In Joshua 20, God had set up *cities of refuge* "among the Israelites, certain cities appointed to secure the safety of such persons as might commit homicide without design. Of these there were three on each side of the Jordan."

We can clearly see that it's Jesus we run to from the enemy and distress of this world. Make Him your refuge and rejoice that He is your stronghold, fortress, hiding place, mainstay, support, safeguard and anchor. An interesting synonym for refuge is *ark*. Didn't Noah find refuge from God's judgment in the ark?

Refuge implies "avoidance, evasion, flight, escape, retreat, departure." When I lived in the mission field for a short time early on in my marriage, my husband's country was at war. He couldn't return home because he would have been taken immediately into the army, even though he had served his time. We lived just an hour or so away from his home, but he had to *avoid* his home altogether. The Lord had made a way of *escape* for his protection. His younger brother and close friend had to flee the country for refuge as did so many others during that time. What a comfort it is knowing "God is our refuge and strength, a very present help in trouble. Therefore we will not fear, even though the earth be removed, and though the mountains be carried into the midst of the sea, though its waters roar and be troubled, though the mountains shake with its swelling. . . . God is in the midst of her, she shall not be moved, God shall help her just at the break of dawn" (Ps. 46:1-5).

I may feel like the enemy is right on my heels in hot pursuit of my life, ready to hunt me down; but I can rejoice because God is greater and He is my refuge from every storm. "O Lord God of Hosts, who is mighty like You, O Lord, Your faithfulness also surrounds You. You rule the raging of the sea; when its waves rise You still them" (Ps. 89:8-9). "In the fear of the Lord there is strong confidence, and His children will have a place of refuge" (Prov. 14:26). "You have been my defense and refuge in the day of trouble" (Ps. 59:16). Run to Him for refuge even now and know He is your hiding place, the anchor of your soul. You are safe, inaccessible from the enemy when you are in the arms of God.

"For you have been a defense for the helpless, a defense for the needy in his distress, a refuge from the storm, a shade from the heat" (Isa. 25:4).

Reasons to Rejoice, Part 2: Rescue

In Your righteousness deliver me and rescue me.
Psalm 71:2

Chapter 22

Our second reason to rejoice is that He is able to rescue. Psalm 71:2 says, "In Your righteousness deliver me and rescue me; incline Your ear to me and save me." We sang this worship song at church this morning: "I called and You answered, and You came to my rescue. And I just want to be where You are. My whole life I place in Your hands. God of mercy, humbly I bow down." Have you felt like you needed to be rescued? Does it ever seem like you're drowning and can hardly get a breath? And as soon as you get a break, the enemy comes in to sow a seed of despair. There's no safer place to be than in His hands. What a comfort it is, knowing that our beloved Savior is so close—as soon as I call He's there.

> His hands that bore the nails on the cross,
> His hands that were pinned to the tree,
> His hands that bled for you and me,
> His hands are able to set us free.

We've all been rescued from the sin that held us prisoners. If you believe in our hearts and confess with your mouth that God has raised Him (Jesus) from the dead, you will be saved. "For with the heart one believes unto righteousness, and with the mouth confession is made unto salvation" (Rom. 10:10). There's a rescuing for my soul that needed to take place when I came to God. But as I walk with God I need to be rescued from myself and the enemy as well. "Rescue the weak and needy; deliver them out of the hand of the wicked" (Ps. 82:4).

Rescue means "to free or deliver from any confinement, violence, danger or evil; to liberate from actual restraint or to remove or withdraw from a state of exposure to evil." Rescue speaks of deliverance, a respite, liberation, redemption, salvation, to set free or save. John 8:36 says, "If the Son sets you free, you will be free indeed." It implies release. If God was able to rescue Daniel from the pit and power of the lion, certainly He is able to deliver me from any pit I may be in and from the roaring lion who seeks to devour me. "He delivers and rescues and performs signs and wonders in heaven and on earth, Who has also delivered Daniel from the power of the lions" (Dan. 6:27). Truly He is a wonder-working God. He delights in the impossible.

Psalm 31:14-15 says, "But as for me, I trust in You, O Lord, I say, 'You are my God.' My times are in Your hand; deliver me from the hand of my enemies and from those who persecute me." If God's hand spans the universe, I'm in good hands. His hand is big enough to rescue me. When we need a helping hand, we can trust in Him to be that ever present help in time of need. Let's not forget that there are scars on those hands that are a constant reminder to us that

He loves us. No matter what! He is with us always. What a joy!

Psalm 6:4 says, "Return, O Lord, rescue my soul; save me because of Your lovingkindness." Verse 9 says, "The Lord has heard my supplication, the Lord receives my prayer." When we cry out, He hears us. We can be confident our plea for help doesn't fall on deaf ears. The psalmist wrote it in the past tense, "He has heard"—there's assurance in his heart. Unlike the Lord, I sometimes wonder if my son really heard me when I called him. Was he truly listening to me? Then there are those times I know he clearly did not hear me at all. That is never true of my heavenly Father. He always hears the cry of His kids.

"The Lord knows how to rescue the godly from trials" (2 Pet. 2:9). Turn to Him; ask Him to come to your rescue. He cannot fail, we have His word. Joshua was able to say, when he was "old and well advanced in years" (Josh. 23:1), "Now behold, today I am going the way of all the earth, and you know in all your hearts and in all your souls that not one word of all the good words which the Lord your God spoke concerning you has failed; all have been fulfilled for you, not one of them has failed" (Josh. 23:14).

What a testimony Joshua gave. Consider what the Lord has done for you and expect Him to do much more. He is the real promise keeper. And He is able to come to my rescue and yours too. Now that's reason to rejoice!

Reasons to Rejoice, Part 3: Rock

You are my rock.
Psalm 71:3

Chapter 23

Our third reason to rejoice is found in Psalm 71:3, "Be to me a rock of habitation to which I may continually come; You have given commandment to save me, for You are my rock and my fortress."

Rock: "In Scripture, figuratively, defense; means of safety; protection; strength; asylum. 2 Samuel 22: 'The Lord is my rock;' firmness, a form or immovable foundation."

Please read Psalm 27—it's one of my all-time favorites. The whole psalm is solid bedrock for our soul. Psalm 27:3 says, "Though an army may encamp against me, my heart shall not fear; though war may rise against me, in this I will be confident." Verse 5: "For in the time of trouble He shall hide me in His pavilion; in the secret place of His tabernacle He shall hide me; He shall set me high upon a rock." "And the rain descended, the floods came, and the winds blew and beat on that house; and it did not fall, for it was founded on the rock" (Matt. 7:25).

"When the enemy comes in like a flood, the Spirit of the Lord will lift up a standard against him" (Isa. 59:19). Our foe is relentless. He won't stop his attacks. He wants to take us out and knock us off our foundation which is Christ. But when we are founded upon the rock, we will be safe and weather the storm. The winds may blow, but he can't touch my soul. "My soul's secure, your promise sure" is a line from a worship song we sing at church. No matter what we face, we have the confidence that "on Christ the solid rock I stand, all other ground is sinking sand." The enemy may attempt to sink my ship, but Jesus is my rock of defense. And like the psalmist we too can sing, "He is my defense; I shall not be moved" (Ps. 62:6). (I can't help but think of Mary Goetz singing this psalm, it's just the best.) Mr. Noah Webster alluded to it in his definition, "The Lord lives, blessed be my rock! Let God be exalted, the rock of my salvation."

God is our rock, our bulwark. (I've always wondered what exactly that meant.) Bulwark: "In fortification, any means of defense, that which secures against the enemy or external annoyance; a screen or shelter." "For You are my rock and fortress; therefore, for Your name's sake, lead me and guide me" (Psalm 31:3).

I pray that knowing God as your rock, you find comfort in Him. May He strengthen you and be your defense from the enemy. As you look to the Lord your rock, may He make you "steadfast, immovable, always abounding in the work of the Lord, knowing that your toil is not in vain in the Lord" (I Cor. 15:58). May you find shelter in the Lord, as you go through the storms of life. He will be faithful to keep and guard and protect you. Just as Paul was kept safe in the midst of a violent typhoon, we can be confident that the Lord will carry us to safe ground as well (Acts 27). Be of good courage, take heart: "For this very night an angel of the God to whom I belong and whom I serve stood before me, saying, 'Do not be afraid Paul'" (Acts 27:23-24). "Paul knew the power of the promise of God's Word" (Terry Walker). What better place to find His strength than in the presence of God and His Word. Rejoice, again I say rejoice!!!

Reasons to Rejoice, Part 4: Reliable

He is utterly reliable.
Psalm 71:6

Chapter 24

"From birth I have relied on You; You brought me forth from my mother's womb. I will ever praise You." We rejoice that "He is utterly reliable" (Ps. 71:6).

Reliance means "rest or repose of mind, resulting from a full belief of the veracity or integrity of a person, or the certainty of a fact; trust; confidence; dependence. We may have perfect reliance on the promises of God; above all things, we rely on the mercy and promises of God." Yes, that is all in the *Noah Webster 1828 Dictionary*. I didn't make it up. There is a peace that comes from the belief that God is who He says He is. The fact that He loves me and died for me causes me to trust His reliability. His promises are sure. I can depend on them and take them to the bank with total confidence. There aren't many things we can have perfect reliance on in this world, but when it comes to God and His promises that is the one place we can rest assured in.

Synonyms for reliable are "sureness, surety, assurance, reliability, absolute, positive, unequivocal, unmistakable, undeniable, unquestionable, indisputable, incontestable, irrefutable, infallible, undoubted, unerring, trustworthy, to be sure." When you think of God in this context doesn't it just cause you to stand in awe of Him and praise His holy name?

We can count on the Lord with absolute certainty and His promises without question. He is completely trustworthy. His character is unmistakable. He who promised is faithful. His mercies are undeniable. His grace is unquestionable. His forgiveness is irrefutable. His wisdom is infallible. His guidance is unerring, better than any GPS the world has to offer. His resurrection is absolutely, positively without doubt. We have a risen Savior and there's an empty tomb to prove it. We can confide in, believe in and place our reliance upon His Word to us, day in and day out.

Jesus said in John 8:26: "He who sent me is reliable, and what I have heard from Him I tell the world." I love Proverbs 3:5 in the Amplified Bible: "Lean on, trust in, and be confident in the Lord with all your heart and mind and do not rely on your own insight or understanding." We clearly see WHO we place our reliance on—God and not ourselves.

I really want to encourage you with this promise from John 16:20: "You will be sorrowful, but your sorrow will be turned into joy." God is able to turn our sorrow into joy. As the Lord takes us through our trials, He wants to give us victory in them. He doesn't want us defeated, discouraged, depressed or sorrowing as those who have no hope. He desires to turn our fears to faith and our worries to prayers, while exchanging our anxiousness for His peace. He takes our fretting and gives us His peace in the midst of turmoil. We must take Him at His word and choose to believe He is who He claims to be: God Almighty, Immanuel, God with us.

After my mom went to be with the Lord, there was a time of grieving. The Lord ministered to me that promise, "You will be sorrowful, but your sorrow will be turned to joy." The room my mom was in the last seven months of her life certainly was a room filled with sorrow as a result of the cancer and its effects on her life. In just two years that very room became a nursery when my husband and I brought home our newborn son from the hospital. Our son's name means "God has filled with joy." In God's miraculous way He turned my sorrow into joy. It was all in His perfect timing. What is causing your heart to sorrow? Give it to Him. Healing takes time. As we have seen, He is our rock and our refuge. He alone is able to rescue us, all the while being completely reliable. There truly is much to rejoice in Him for.

Reasons to Rejoice, Part 5: Righteousness

Your righteousness
reaches to the skies, O God,
You who have done great things.
Who, O God, is like You?
Psalm 71:19

Chapter 25

As we continue with our reasons to rejoice we come to *His righteousness.* We have been declared righteous through Jesus' shed blood on the cross. His righteousness has been imputed to our account.

Righteous "denotes one who is holy in heart and observant of the divine commands in practice." (It's interesting that when Jesus came He fulfilled the commandments of the Law, living a perfect life because we never could.) Righteous "is used chiefly in theology and applies to God, to His testimonies and to His saints." Righteousness is "purity of heart, as used in the Scriptures and theology, in which it is nearly equivalent to holiness. Applied to God, the perfection or holiness of his nature; faithfulness." We know Jesus is the pure, spotless Lamb of God, holy and perfect in nature.

This leads us to our fifth reason to rejoice: His righteousness. It is so important to lay this foundation for us to better understand what His righteousness entails and affords us. If righteousness is "nearly equivalent with holiness," we need a proper grasp of what holiness really means.

The sense of the word *holy* is "whole, entire, or perfect in a moral sense. Hence, pure in heart, temper or dispositions. Free from sin and sinful affections. Applied to the Supreme Being, holy signifies PERFECTLY PURE, IMMACULATE and complete in moral character." Jesus is "perfectly pure, immaculate"—there is no one like our God! "Man is more or less holy as his heart is more or less sanctified, or purified from evil dispositions. We call a man holy when his heart is conformed in some degree to the image of God and his life is regulated by the divine precepts. Hence, holy is used as nearly synonymous with good, pious and godly."

Wow, where do I begin? All I can think of is our God is so incredibly holy and majestic, He takes my breath away and I just long to worship Him all the more for the beauty of His holiness. God is holy and I am not, apart from Him and the influence of His Holy Spirit upon my life.

Romans 4:22, speaking of Abraham, says, "And therefore 'it was accounted to him for righteousness.'" What was accounted to him for righteousness? His faith in God's promise. Abraham simply believed God and was justified by his faith. "For He made Him who knew no sin to be sin for us, that we might become the righteousness of God in Him" (2 Cor. 5:21). We see Jesus is perfectly pure, immaculate and we've been made holy "to the degree that He has my heart and is conforming it to the image of God."

David knew this principle as he penned Psalm 51. The man after God's own heart prayed, "Wash me thoroughly from my iniquity, and cleanse me from my sin. Purge me with hyssop, and I shall be clean; wash me and I shall me whiter than snow. Create in me a clean heart, O God, and renew a steadfast spirit within me" (Ps. 51:2, 7, 10). Even though David sinned, his heart was continually moving in the direction of desiring to be holy as God is holy. He repented and knew that, through the sacrifice of the blood of a lamb, the Lord was able to make Him whiter than snow. We can rejoice that by God's grace we are declared righteous in His sight.

Reasons to Rejoice, Part 6: Restore

Though You have made me see troubles,
many and bitter, You will restore my life again.
Psalm 71:20

Chapter 26

Looking ahead to the Kingdom Age, it will truly be glorious: no more death and no more sin and the sorrow it brings. It will be a total joy to be with Jesus for all of eternity. But what about now? What if you find yourself in a valley? How can you be fruitful there?

"Thus says the Lord: 'Because the Syrians have said, "The Lord is God of the hills, but He is not God of the valleys," therefore I will deliver all this great multitude into your hand, and you shall know that I am the Lord'" (1 Kings 20:28).

The Syrians thought if they moved the battle to the valley they would win over Israel thinking Jehovah was only the God of the mountain top. Boy, were they wrong. Verse 29 says, "And the Children of Israel killed one hundred thousand foot soldiers of the Syrians in one day." There was the belief in those days that gods were localized, similar to ancient Egyptian beliefs. We know our God is not limited to one mountain. He is the God of the valley too. The Lord allows us to go through valleys so that the world will see He is God of our lives, through thick and thin. It's in the valleys that God reveals His goodness and grace and faithfulness for the world to witness.

Once again, we rejoice in Him. He is our joy. Psalm 71:20: "Though you have made me see troubles, many and bitter, you will RESTORE my life again; from the depths of the earth you will again bring me up." It sounds like the psalmist had his own valley to deal with and perhaps found himself in a pit of despair, but he sees the *God of the valley* and the hope surges in his soul that God will restore him.

Restore: "This is a compound of 're' and the root of store-story-history." Stop there. *History, story . . .* your life, your testimony is *His story.* Think about it. He is the author and finisher of your faith (Heb. 12:2). "He's writing the story of your life and the good news is, the story isn't over. It may be Chapter 5 or 10 or 25 or even 50, but God is not through with you. The book isn't finished yet" (Terry Walker).

Restore is also "to replace, to return, to heal, to cure, to repair, to rebuild, to revive, to resuscitate, to bring back to life." Jesus has restored my soul, my relationship with God the Father. A person that is unconscious needs CPR to be resuscitated. They are on the verge of death. How much more did Jesus breathe life into our lives when we were dead in our sins? He revived us and brought us back to life spiritually. It also means "to renew or re-establish after interruption as peace is restored. Friendship between the parties is restored." There was an *interruption* or *break* between us and God because of sin, but now we have peace with God through Jesus

our Lord. Abraham was called the *Friend of God.*
Jesus said in John 15:14, "You are My friends if you
do whatever I command you." What a blessing the
friendship is that we have with God. He is the friend
that sticks closer than a brother (Prov. 18:24)!

Synonyms for *restoration* are "rehabilitation,
renovation, reproduction." (Yes, I'm presently under
construction—a work in progress—and so are you!)
His life is daily being *reproduced* in us. As we walk
through the valleys He's giving us more of His love,
more of his joy and more patience. Restoration also
speaks of *rebirth*: Jesus declared, "I tell you the truth,
no one can see the kingdom of God unless he is born
again. . . . Flesh gives birth to flesh, but the Spirit gives
birth to spirit. You should not be surprised at my
saying, 'You must be born again'" (John 3:3, 6-7).
This synonym amazes me: resurrection. Apart from
Jesus raising from the dead, our hope would be in
vain and there would be no restoration. He is the
resurrection and the Life (John 11).

With all that the Lord has done for us in restoring
our friendship with God and giving us new life,
ponder His Word and may it cause a spring of joy to
well up within your soul. Rejoice in Him always.

Reasons to Rejoice, Part 7: Revive

From the depths of the earth
You will again bring me up.
Psalm 71:20

Chapter 27

"You who have shown me many troubles and distresses will revive me again, and will bring me up again from the depths of the earth" (Psalm 71:20). What precious hope lies within this promise. It's a promise that we can take to the bank with confidence, because He who promised is faithful!

Revive: "To return to life, to recover from a state of neglect, oblivion, obscurity or depression; to refresh with joy and hope." For something or someone to need revival, it would seem that life or hope has been lost at some point. I think of a person in cardiac arrest. They are on the verge of death. Their heart stops. The doctor brings out the crash cart and attempts to shock the heart back to its regular beat, seeking to revive the person. Hopefully the patient responds and they recover. We have been touched by the master physician Jesus Christ. He has brought us back from death to life. We were lost in sin, walking in oblivion apart from God. For some it was a time of hopelessness and depression. But thanks be to God who always leads us in triumph. I think of

Resurrection Sunday and the wonderful victory we celebrate in Christ over sin, death and the enemy.

> Up from the grave He arose,
> With a mighty triumph o'er His foes,
> He arose a Victor from the dark domain,
> And He lives forever, with His saints to reign.
> He arose! He arose!
> Hallelujah! Christ arose!
> ("Christ Arose" by Robert Lowry)

Jesus has breathed life into our souls. "If anyone is in Christ, he is a new creation; old things have passed away; behold, all things have become new" (2 Cor. 5:17). Our lives were in ruins before He saved us, like a pile of rubble on a construction site. The chorus to an old worship song rings true: "Ruined lives are why You died on Calvary, Your touch is what I long for, You have given life to me." Praise the Lord for the life we have in Him.

Our hope as Christians is found in the cross and the empty tomb. Our sins are forgiven at the cross, but if the story ended there with Jesus still on the cross the victory would not be complete. "If there is no resurrection of the dead, then Christ is not risen. And if Christ is not risen, then our preaching is empty and your faith is also empty. . . . And if Christ is not risen, your faith is futile; you are still in your sins! . . . But now Christ is risen from the dead, and has become the firstfruits of those who have fallen asleep" (1 Cor. 15:13-14, 17, 20). We have a risen Savior who rose again on the third day, bringing us the greatest hope of revival.

Synonyms for *revival* are reproduction, resurrection and resuscitation. *Reproduction:* we are *born again* when we come to Him. A new life is birthed in us, Christ in us the hope of glory! *Resurrection:* Jesus said, "I am the resurrection and the life. He who believes in Me, though he may die, he shall live. And whoever lives and believes in Me shall never die. Do you believe this?" (John 11:25-26). *Resuscitate*, like a person who has fainted and is unconscious. We too needed the Lord to breathe life into our soul. Other synonyms are recovery, repair, to mend, to remodel, reclaim, reform and improve. Our lives are like a construction site. We are all in the process of a remodel. From day to day the Lord is transforming us. I love this verse that David penned, "That our sons may be as plants grown up in their youth; that our daughters may be as pillars, sculptured in palace style" (Ps. 144:12). It speaks to me of growth and fruitfulness, with Jesus as general contractor overseeing the design project. May God take our lives and bring those needed repairs—mending our hearts and reclaiming our souls for Him.

Jesus said, "I chose you and appointed you that you should go and bear fruit, and that your fruit should remain" (John 15:16). Each one of us has been called to live a fruitful life. Paul prayed for the believers in Colossae, "That you may walk (live and conduct yourselves) in a manner worthy of the Lord, fully pleasing to Him and desiring to please Him in all things, bearing fruit in every good work and steadily growing and increasing in and by the knowledge of God [with fuller, deeper, and clearer insight,

119

acquaintance and recognition]. [We pray] that you may be invigorated and strengthened with all power according to the might of His glory, [to exercise] every kind of endurance and patience (perseverance and forbearance) with joy" (Col. 1:10-11).

We need to be *more full* of the Lord. Fuller in our knowledge of Him doesn't mean just head knowledge but heart knowledge. Knowing Him by experience as we walk with Him each day through the tough times and heartaches of life. Where do we grow the most as Christians? In the valleys of life and in the fiery furnace. When arrows are flying our way and we find ourselves in the thick of the battle, we cry out for help. It's there we draw near to God and He draws near to us. I know the cry of my kids when they are in trouble. And believe me if they're hurt or in need, I come running. How much more will Jesus revive us when we call out to Him? He is faithful to respond to us with hope and comfort when we ask for it. He is the true joy giver! Our living hope! He alone can quicken our hearts to the right beat and breathe new life in us when we are about to sink. David prayed, "Revive me in Your ways. . . . My soul clings to the dust; revive me according to Your word" (Ps. 119:37 & 25).

Wherever you find yourself today, humble yourself before God. We have a High Priest who sympathizes with our weaknesses (Heb. 4:15). Look to Him and He will give you joy for the journey and the hope of heaven to finish well. "After two days He will revive us; on the third day He will restore us" (Hosea 6:2). It's been more than two thousand years since Jesus died and rose again. With the Lord a day is as a thousand years (2 Peter 3:8). On the third day He rose again. We are closer than ever to his return. One day very soon we will be reunited with Him. Two days doesn't seem so long. No one knows the hour or day of His return but the Father. The days we are living in tell us that Jesus' coming is near. May that truth revive our hearts in the darkest of times, causing us to place our hope in Him. Rejoice that He is able to do exceedingly abundantly above all that we ask or think. Revival is possible in Him.

"For this is what the high and lofty One says—He who lives forever, whose name is holy: 'I live in a high and holy place, but also with him who is contrite and lowly in spirit, to revive the spirit of the lowly and to revive the heart of the contrite'" (Isa. 57:15).

Reasons to Rejoice, Part 8: Redeemed

My lips will shout for joy when I sing praise to You—I, whom You have redeemed.
Psalm 71:23

Chapter 28

This weekend my son is at his first junior high winter camp with church. It's been some years since I was in junior high and went to Forest Home or Hume Lake. The songs have changed over the years, but the Lord is the same yesterday, today and forever. I remember a song I used to sing when I was in junior high youth group years ago: "I've been redeemed . . . by the blood of the Lamb . . . I've been redeemed by the blood of the Lamb, the Holy Ghost says I am, all my sins are washed away, I've been redeemed!" Our 8th reason to rejoice is: We've been redeemed!

Whether we realize it or not, we were at one time held captive by the enemy. We desperately needed to be liberated from his grip. Fortunately, the ransom was paid in full. It says in 1 Peter that we were not redeemed by the blood of bulls or goats but by the precious blood of Jesus. His blood was shed, releasing us from the bondage of Satan's hold upon our lives. And now we have been set free to live for Him.

Once a year the High Priest would go into the Holy of Holies and offer a sacrifice to make atonement for the sins of the people. The problem with the Old Testament sacrifices was that they only *covered* sin. They never fully *removed* sin. All the sacrifices pointed to our Great High Priest Jesus Christ who would take away sin once and for all. "For it is not possible that the blood of bulls and goats could take away sins" (Heb. 10:4). Why was there the need for animal sacrifices? Sin had to be dealt with. "And according to the law almost all things are purified with blood, and without the shedding of blood there is no remission" (Heb. 9:22). When Adam sinned, it brought a separation to the fellowship that He and the Lord once had. God is holy and His eyes are too pure to behold iniquity (Hab. 1:13). "The wages of sin is death, but the gift of God is eternal life in Christ Jesus our Lord" (Rom. 6:23).

The Latin word *redimo* from which we get our English word *redeem* means to obtain or purchase. To *redeem* is to ransom, liberate, rescue from captivity or bondage; to free by making atonement. That's exactly what Jesus came to do: bring AT-ONE-MENT! The only way for us to be *at one* with Him was for Him to die in our place. What fellowship is there between holiness and sin? The perfect friendship that once existed between Adam and God had been lost in the garden. As a result, sin kept us captives of the enemy. "So Christ was offered once to bear the sins of many. To those who eagerly wait for Him He will appear a second time, apart from sin, for salvation" (Heb. 9:28). The Old Testament priests had to atone for their sin as they offered sacrifices for the people, but Jesus is our Holy and High Priest. "But now, once at the end of the ages, He has appeared to put away sin by the sacrifice of himself" (Heb. 9:26). Under Old Testament law sin was merely covered, but through Jesus it's been removed. Our Redeemer has reclaimed our lives, giving us a great reason to rejoice.

It is through our personal relationship with Christ that we experience being rescued, delivered and redeemed. Our last reason to rejoice in this section is found in Psalm 71:12. The psalmist cried out to the Lord, "Be not far from me, O God; come quickly, O my God, to help me." I'm so grateful that the Creator of the universe reveals himself to us as a loving Father who longs to be reunited with his children. A relative is a person connected by blood. We have been connected to Jesus by His blood and now we are in the family of God. Jesus is our kinsman redeemer. The cross of Christ connects us to the Father, bridging the gap that once existed between ourselves and God.

Eternal life isn't just something we wait for as we look to heaven. It begins the moment we enter into a relationship with God. "Now this is eternal life: that they may know You, the only true God, and Jesus Christ, whom you have sent" (John 17:3). Having a relationship with God is unique when comparing Christianity to religion. Christianity is centered on the cross. Religion centers on what man has to do to reach God. Christ reached down to man. Religion says, "Do, do, do." Christianity says, "Done, done, done." IT IS FINISHED! All that is left for us to do is enjoy Jesus, love Him and respond to His gift of grace. My kids don't have to try and earn my love; it's a given, simply because I'm their Mom. It's all about relationship. God has called us into this wonderful body of Christ, the Family of God, where together with other believers we grow in our relationship with Him and each other. He's our heavenly Father. I have a *relationship* with a true prince—the Prince of Peace—who has swept me off my feet.

There are so many blessings this special relationship affords us. We can run to Him for refuge. When we call on Him to rescue us, He is there. In those times of weakness, He is our rock. Each day He reveals himself to be utterly reliable. I have relied on God's promises for years to carry me through the storms of life. Not once has He failed. In most relationships you hope that each party will give equally. But in our relationship with Jesus, He gave everything. He did it all and we simply receive by faith His righteousness over our lives. When Abraham was about to enter into a covenant with God, it was the custom of the day for both parties to walk in the middle of the slain animals signifying that God was dead serious about the covenant. But while Abraham waited for God to show up, he fell asleep. And it was while Abraham was sleeping that God came and sealed the deal. We can count on the Lord to revive us knowing He's done it in the past. We have many reasons to rejoice in Him. May each one of these "R" words remind you to rejoice forevermore because of all He's done. He really is remarkable! Add it to your list.

The Greatest of All Reasons to Rejoice

In the same region there were some
shepherds staying out in the fields and
keeping watch over their flock by night.
And an angel of the Lord suddenly stood
before them, and the glory of the Lord shone around
them; and they were terribly frightened. But the
angel said to them, "Do not be afraid; for behold,
I bring you good news of great joy which will be for
all the people; for today in the city of David
there has been born for you a Savior,
who is Christ the Lord."
Luke 2:8-11

Chapter 29

Is there anything greater than our dear Savior's birth? He's the love of our lives. He's the reason we get up in the morning. He is the hope that lies within us. He is the anchor of our soul. He is our absolute everything. For Christians, celebrating His birth is the highlight of the year, next to Resurrection Sunday. Our country and much of the world celebrate Christmas, but do they rejoice over *Christ* who is the true reason for the season? Sadly, no. Much of their celebration is not because of Jesus and the Good News He brings or the great joy He offers. Yet, He still came for *all* people, knowing many would reject

Him. But, for us who love Him dearly, let's look at this extraordinary birth and the great joy it brings.

Savior: "One that saves or preserves; but properly applied only to Jesus Christ, the Redeemer, who has opened the way to everlasting salvation by His obedience and death and who is therefore called *the* Savior, by way of distinction, the Savior of men, the Savior of the world."

Why did God send his Son to be the Savior of the world? The honest truth is that we needed saving. We needed a redeemer; one who would redeem us from the curse of sin. "In Adam's fall, we sinned all" (*The New England Primer*, 1777 edition). Sin is the basis of all our problems. Noah Webster defines sin as "native depravity of heart, that want (lack) of conformity of heart to the divine will, that corruption of nature or deterioration of the moral character of man." Sin is basically to "offend against right, against men or society; to trespass; to depart voluntarily from the path of duty prescribed by God to man." "For all have sinned, and come short of the glory of God" (Rom. 3:23).

We have all sinned, "departed from the path prescribed by God." Sin separates us from a Holy God. And the Bible says there is a consequence to sin. "For the wages of sin is death, but the gift of God is eternal life in Christ Jesus our Lord" (Rom. 6:23). The Good News is we've been sent a Savior. He came to offer us His free gift of salvation. Where sin separated us, His birth unites us back to God when we receive the gift. Jesus openly said, "I give them eternal life" (John 10:28). There is no better gift in the entire world! "And this is eternal life, that they may know You, the only true God, and Jesus Christ whom you have sent" (John 17:3). It will take all of eternity to truly know God's love and grace and kindness, and it begins now.

The continuation of that Good News is found in the grace of God. "For by grace you have been saved through faith, and that not of yourselves; it is the gift of God" (Eph. 2:8). In the heart of God is love beyond imagination for his people. The message is wonderful beyond words and the greatest joy of my heart. God's grace is "free, ready, quick, willing and prompt." The Gospel is all wrapped up in "this history of the birth, life, actions, death, resurrection, ascension, and doctrines of Jesus Christ." What great joy there is in knowing that the Lord loves us, and His free gift has been sent to us in the birth of His Son. I can't open the gift for you and accept it on your behalf. Each one of us must make that personal choice to accept His love and Good News. The Savior we celebrate, the baby Jesus we remember and worship at Christmas, is the creator and sustainer of the universe. The creator became our Savior.

To think that our God—the King of Kings and Lord of Lords, the King of Glory—left his throne and took on human flesh is truly amazing. He came as an innocent, helpless, dependent baby. People say babies are innocent, but it doesn't take long for that baby to turn into a 2-year-old and demand its own way. That's when you find out they aren't really innocent after all; they too have a sin nature. But our Jesus was entirely innocent, He who knew no sin became sin for us. He who is called an "ever present help in time of need" came needing the help of his mother. Jehovah, who spoke the world into existence, learned to speak. God, whose hand spans the universe, was cradled in His mother's arms. El Shaddai, God Almighty had to learn to walk. Jehovah Jireh, the Lord who provides, looked to his mother and Joseph to provide for Him shelter and safety. He came and dwelt among us as that perfect baby with tiny, little hands which could barely wrap around his mother's finger. How did God confine himself to an infant? I have no idea. But I do know He came for every person in all the masses of humanity throughout all the ages of history for one reason: He came to die. He saw you and simply couldn't live without you. "God would rather die than live without you" (Max Lucado, *Emmanuel: The Glory of Christmas*).

It's interesting that in our world today being *spiritual* is almost popular and *in*. Yet not one religious leader through the ages can claim the title Savior. Not Mohammad, not Buddha, not anyone but Jesus Christ. Why is that? Because they neglect to deal with the problem of sin. They have no answer or solution for it. They attempt to reach God by their own efforts and works. And their message is one of works. They don't have *good news* to share.

GOD ALONE CAME DOWN to mankind. His name is Emmanuel, God with us. Christianity is not a religion; it's a relationship with God through the person Jesus Christ, God incarnate. *Incarnate* comes from the Latin words *in* and *carno* meaning "flesh, to clothe with flesh, embodied in flesh, as the incarnate

Son of God." Make no mistake, Jesus is God in the flesh.

It may not be Christmas time when you are reading this, but the message is not bound to a month or a single day of the year. May this Good News truly bring you great joy no matter what time of year it is. This good news is *great*, as in "large in bulk or dimensions; denoting more magnitude or extension than something else, or beyond that which is usual." (This is so great; the *bulk* of it is so enormous that Costco doesn't even carry it.) *Great* is also "being of extended length or breadth." God's gift of salvation, our greatest reason for rejoicing, is seen in the cross where Jesus displayed his undying love for us. Paul prayed that the believers in Ephesus would be able "to comprehend with all the saints what is the breadth and length and height and depth, and to know the love of Christ which passes knowledge"(Eph. 3:18-19). What could be greater than His love that reaches to the heavens and His mercies that are deeper than the sea? This Great News is of vast power and excellence and supreme above all else.

May you embrace this great joy for yourself today. Rejoice in Him and the free gift of grace He brings. He is Savior, Messiah, Redeemer, Deliverer and King. Worship Him. Follow Him closely as the wise men did. Spread the Good News like the shepherds did that very night with haste. Continue to ponder in your heart as Mary did the wonders of our Savior. Jesus came as that precious gift of God to a lowly manger to ultimately live and dwell in the hearts of man. Rejoice! It's no wonder that we sing "Joy to the World" during Christmas, for truly joy was born to us in our beloved Savior on Christmas morning. The joy of knowing God personally, the joy of having your sin forgiven and slate wiped clean, and the joy of knowing one day we will be in heaven with Him forever. May your heart sing unto Him, "Joy to the world, the Lord has come, let earth receive her King. Let every heart prepare Him room, and heaven and nature sing!" To Him be the glory, the honor and praise, both now and forever! Amen.

In Me You May Have Peace

These things I have spoken to you,
that in Me you may have peace. In the
world you will have tribulation; but be of good
cheer, I have overcome the world.
John 16:33

Chapter 30

"You will keep him in perfect peace, whose mind is stayed on You, because he trusts in You" (Isa. 26:3). "The eternal God is your refuge, and underneath are the everlasting arms; He will thrust out the enemy from before you" (Deut. 33:27). "The beloved of the Lord shall dwell in safety by Him, who shelters him all the day long; and he shall dwell between His shoulders" (Deut. 33:12). "'Not by might nor by power, but by My Spirit,' says the Lord of Hosts" (Zech. 4:6).

"Have you not known? Have you not heard? The everlasting God, the Lord, the creator of the ends of the earth, neither faints nor is weary. His understanding is unsearchable. He gives power to the weak, and to those who have no might He increases strength. Even the youths shall faint and be weary, and the young men shall utterly fall, but those who wait on the Lord shall renew their strength; they shall mount up with wings like eagles, they shall run and not be weary, they shall walk and not faint" (Isa. 40:28-31).

What do all these verses have in common? They each are a word from the Living God who speaks peace and strength over His children. When we are weak, He is strong. When we are at our end, He carries us through to victory. When we need power, He is there, ready to come to our aid and fill us to overflowing.

Peace. Just the very word brings a sigh of relief to our souls. As a people individually and as a nation corporately, we long for peace within our borders. Without God's peace there is unrest and turmoil that can haunt us to our very core. Where do I find lasting peace? How do I keep it once I find it?

First, what is real *peace*? "In a general sense, a state of quiet or tranquility; freedom from disturbance or agitation; freedom from war with a foreign nation; freedom from internal commotion; freedom from agitation or disturbances by the passions, as from fear, terror, anger, anxiety, or the like; harmony; a state of reconciliation between parties at variance."

For the Christian, there is the *peace of God* and *peace with God*. Apart from God there is no true peace. For us to find that "freedom from disturbance or internal commotion," we must turn to the Prince of Peace who alone can bring a truce to the war waged within our soul. Once I confess I'm a sinner and receive His gift of salvation by faith through Jesus Christ, my sins are forgiven and the war is over. I'm now *reconciled* to God, and where sin separated that fellowship there is now *harmony* between us and our

Creator. We have been called to peace (1 Cor. 7:15).

"For He himself is our peace, who has made both one, and has broken down the middle wall of separation, having abolished in His flesh the enmity, that is, the law of commandments contained in ordinances, so as to create in himself one new man from the two, thus making peace, and that He might reconcile them both to God in one body through the cross, thereby putting to death the enmity. And He came and preached peace to you who were afar off and to those who were near. For through Him we both have access by one Spirit to the Father" (Eph. 2:14-18).

There is only one place where we are able to find the *peace of God*. It's the place most people try to avoid at all cost: the cross. "For God was pleased to have all His fullness dwell in Him, and through Him to reconcile to himself all things, whether things on earth or in heaven, by making peace through His blood, shed on the cross" (Col. 1:19-20).

I'm so grateful for that reconciliation of Christ on the cross which has freed me from the fear of being eternally separated from God. Knowing I'm forgiven because He was forsaken humbles me, but it calms that anxiousness within. Nothing can separate me from the love of God. We are told in Philippians 4:6-7, "Do not be anxious about anything, but in everything, by prayer and petition, with thanksgiving, present your requests to God. And the peace of God, which transcends all understanding, will guard your hearts and your minds in Christ Jesus."

God's peace will hush every anxious thought. His

peace will calm the storm that rages within our minds. What is it that tries to steal your peace? Is it a fear of the future or fear of the unknown? Bring all those cares and concerns to the cross, lay them at His feet and rest in His love for you. The enemy's strategy is to wage war in our mind and thoughts. His tactics are to sow seeds of doubt and fear. Or he just flat out lies. When we are under fire and those fiery darts are flying into our camp, we must take those lies or doubts and, like a cowboy, lasso them captive. Just like a soldier who's captured the enemy and places him under arrest. We need to train ourselves to this discipline. As we do, the enemy will be silenced and the panic we feel will turn to peace.

In those moments we must: *P*urpose in our minds to *E*stablish what is true. Is this threat fact or fiction? Take it to God's throne of grace and *A*ccess the mercy and help He offers in our time of need. *C*all to Him: "Call to Me, and I will answer you, and show you great and mighty things, which you do not know" (Jer. 33:3). "*E*nter into His gates with thanksgiving, and into His courts with praise" (Ps. 100:4). If we will take these steps, we will find our peace in Him (John 16:33).

*P*urpose + *E*stablish + *A*ccess + *C*all + *E*nter = PEACE

"Now may the God of hope fill you with all joy and peace in believing, that you may abound in hope by the power of the Holy Spirit" (Rom. 15:13).

The Peace of God

The Lord will give strength to His people;
the Lord will bless His people with peace.
Psalm 29:11

Chapter 31

I hope as we travel along this journey together you are finding yourself filled to overflowing with God's Spirit in your life. When we take our eyes off ourselves and fix our mind onto the Lord, He does a wonderful thing in our heart. Just like a tailor would alter an outfit, He is altering our lives to be less carnal and more spiritual. Such is the Christian life: a walk of faith, continually moving towards the things of the Spirit. The Lord desires to take us deeper in our walk with Him. He's filling us daily with more of His love, more joy and more peace. As He increases, we decrease. We still live in this fallen world, but it is not our final destination. Yes, there are tribulations, distresses of life and severe afflictions that weigh on us. Sometimes we can feel rather beaten up by the world and the enemy's attacks. It would be nice if we were able to get a break from his lies and tactics, but he never takes a vacation. Yet this promise of the Lord has so much to offer us. It is like a faithful recipe. We all have our favorite meals to cook that we always go back to. We know them by heart, for they are tried and true: chili, enchiladas, lasagna are always a winner in my house. The words of Jesus are ever faithful, tried and true. He offers us his peace in the midst of our pain. He gives us hope that the victory is won. Jesus says, "These things I have spoken to you, that in Me you may have peace. In the world you will have tribulation; but be of good cheer, I have overcome the world" (John 16:33).

As a child of God we've been shown the greatest favor through God's Son. His grace and peace have been made available to us, to bless us and prosper us. I'm not talking out the false teaching of prosperity doctrine that says it's God's will that I'm wealthy, not at all. *Prosper* simply means to grow and increase and to thrive. Is it the Lord's will that we grow spiritually as Christians? Certainly! As a parent I love to watch my kids mature and develop. Our heavenly Father desires the best for His kids. "For it is God who works in you both to will and to do for His good pleasure" (Phil. 2:13). If we are not growing, increasing in faith, expanding our understanding of His Word or experiencing Him personally, then we are probably shriveling up spiritually. God's peace is vital to our spiritual growth. I long to be that well watered garden found in Isaiah 58:11. I have hanging on my staircase wall a beautiful tapestry of a garden with a fountain in the center. Surrounding the fountain are magnificent sprays of colorful flowers and towering trees. It's just the place you'd like to relax for afternoon tea, just to take in all the beauty of God's creation. As the award-winning gardener, Jesus comes to our life enjoying His creation. "For we are His workmanship, created in Christ Jesus for good works, which God prepared beforehand that we should walk in them" (Eph. 2:10). When God's Peace fills our hearts it's like another flower added to our garden.

As we enter this garden, there are four aspects of peace we will discover. First, who holds the peace? "Peace is found in Me," Jesus said. Without God's forgiveness for sin, there is no possibility for peace in our hearts. I'm always saddened when I hear of actors and actresses who, by the world's standards, *have it all* but in reality are so empty. They try to fill that void in their life with possessions that don't satisfy. They go from person to person, seeking to be filled. And sadly some have taken their own life because the emptiness consumes them. The one thing they lack is peace with God, the forgiveness for their sin.

Second, what good is this peace? "'For I know the plans I have for you,' declares the Lord, 'plans to prosper you and not to harm you, plans to give you hope and a future'" (Jer. 29:11). The peace of God offers us hope for our future. It assures us that the Lord is on our side. He desires that we thrive and grow and increase in the things of the Spirit. He allows the attacks that come our way to sharpen and strengthen us. When the Children of Israel returned from exile and were attempting to rebuild the temple, the enemy was relentless with his attacks. He tried fear, frustration, accusations and lies to try and stop the work. He even succeeded for sixteen years. Our adversary goes about like a roaring lion seeking whom he may devour. But greater is He that is in us than he that is in the world. There are many things we can learn to live without, but God's peace is not one of them. His peace carries us through to the finish line of life.

Third, where do we access this peace? "Let us then approach the throne of grace with confidence, so that we may receive mercy and find grace to help us in our time of need" (Heb. 4:16). Jesus says, "In Me you will find peace" (John 16:33). As we were in worship this morning at church, so many of the songs we sang had that common thread of being in His presence. Where the Spirit of the Lord is there is liberty. As we access His presence we are freed from our fears, the power of the enemy and our flesh. It's there that we find the satisfaction we long for and strength for the day. May His peace consume us from the inside out!

Last, why is the enemy always attempting to rob us of our peace? If he can steal my peace he knows I'm vulnerable to his threats. His lies and fear tactics are like arrows that descend upon our minds hoping to infiltrate our thoughts and steal our peace. God's peace is that shield for our soul against the enemy. It's when my peace is gone and panic sets in that I start to be fearful. We may feel like a little lost lamb separated from its shepherd. Our Good Shepherd is always near no matter what the enemy says. Knowing the Lord has a plan and purpose for allowing the things that come our way is a great comfort to our hearts. The next time the enemy comes in to steal your peace remember 2 Chronicles 20:15, "Do not be afraid nor dismayed because of this great multitude, for the battle is not yours, but God's." You may feel like Jehoshaphat, "For we have no power against this great multitude that is coming against us; nor do we know what to do, but our eyes are upon You"(2 Chron. 20:12). The good news is that we don't have power to combat the enemy but Jesus does. Keep your eyes on Him and may He be your peace in the thick of the battle.

During Grace Ann's years in the special education system, some of the hardest trials for me were those IEP (Independent Education Plan) meetings with the teacher, principal, speech therapist and occupational therapist. I dreaded them. I already knew how far behind she was, they didn't need to remind me and show me all the test results, but they did. Whenever I had an IEP coming up, I would ask friends to pray because I didn't want to break down and cry in front of everyone. I knew the Lord had Grace Ann on His timetable, not theirs, and certainly not mine. The Lord was so faithful to give me His peace that passed my understanding, especially when I knew He was calling me to homeschool her. They told me she really needed one-on-one help, so I suggested an aide for her in school. "Well, we can't do that," they told me. All the while, the Lord was tapping me on the shoulder and telling me, "One-on-one. I can help you with that. Don't be afraid. I'll be with you." He gave me peace that enveloped my greatest fears.

For He Himself Is Our Peace

You will keep him in perfect peace,
whose mind is stayed on You,
because he trusts in You.
Isaiah 26:3

Chapter 32

What a gift and blessing the peace of God is to our heart and soul. It's the anchor that keeps us from going adrift in the storms of life. "The Lord will give strength to His people; the Lord will bless His people with peace" (Psalm 29:11). The Latin word from which we get our English word *peace* actually means "to press or to stop." We learned in the previous chapter that peace is "freedom from internal commotion, disturbance or agitation." What happens when we lose our peace? It's a scary thought. If God blesses His people with peace, can it be taken away or really lost? Let's look at Job's life.

Job was a man of piety. "In principle, piety is a compound of veneration or reverence of the Supreme Being and love of His character. In practice, piety is the exercise of these affections in obedience to His will and devotion to His service." We certainly see in Job's life obedience to the will of God and devotion to His service. He was considered blameless and upright by God. We're told he feared God and shunned evil (Job 1:1-5).

Job is a man with a powerful testimony—"the greatest man among all the people of the East" (Job 1:3). He was prosperous materially but, even more so, rich in faith. He had an object of his faith in sight and his aim was to please God. We see further in his life his intention and great resolve.

Job was a man of purpose. He purposed in his heart to put God first. He's an Old Testament example of the Matthew 6:33 principle: "But seek first the kingdom of God and His righteousness, and all these things shall be added to you." Daily he got up early in the morning to offer a burnt offering for each of his ten kids. This was a great sacrifice not only in reality—10 burnt offerings—but a sacrifice of his time, giving up his sleep and not giving into his flesh.

We also see that Job was a worshipper. He praised God with his obedience and devotion to the Lord in good times and in bad times. What greater testimony do we have of one who praises God in the midst of his suffering? "Blessed be the name of the Lord" (Job 1:21).

Lastly, we see Job was a man of passion. We tend to think of passion and love as being synonymous, and that is partly true. But the Latin word *passio* really means "to suffer." Remember the movie *The Passion of the Christ*? The word *passion* refers "emphatically to the last suffering of the Savior." There is no doubt as we read Job's story that he suffered greatly and endured unimaginable loss, all in one day. Passion also means "that impression or effect of an external agent upon a body, that which is suffered or received." The Lord allowed "an external agent," Satan, to come to Job and wreak havoc. Job had already lost his ten children, his servants, his financial wealth and then his own health. Which brings us to Job's greatest loss. Job himself declares, "I have NO PEACE, no quietness; I have no rest, but only turmoil" (Job 3:26). He was a man who had lost his peace on top of everything else. And it brought trouble to his heart.

Turmoil is "a disturbance; to be in commotion; to weary; a harassing labor." Synonyms for turmoil are "disorder" (certainly his world was turned upside down); "confusion, disarray, chaos, an uproar, agitation, and turbulence" (like when you're in a plane and all of a sudden things get shaky and you literally feel like you're going to drop from the sky— you're going down fast). Other synonyms are "restlessness, palpitation, and storm." Have you ever felt like your heart was racing as panic sets in, and the storm within you is raging out of control like an F-5 hurricane sweeping across your life? In that moment all you long for is God's peace to calm your heart and soul.

Some of you may be going through a time of turmoil—your peace is gone. It may be physically, financially, emotionally or even spiritually, and you are just spent. It could be the pain of a parent as they deal with a child who has autism or another special need. Whenever we find ourselves in those times and the turmoil takes the place of our peace we must, like David, "seek peace and pursue it" (Ps. 34:14). Remember, peace signifies "to press or to stop." Jesus was in the garden of Gethsemane which means "olive press." Where do we turn to seek peace? The Prince of Peace who was *pressed* beyond measure as He prayed in the garden, "Not My will, but Thy will be done." So great was He *pressed* that He sweat great drops of blood. Jesus endured the crushing weight of our sin to purchase our peace. The word *press* means to squeeze or to crush, but it also means to embrace closely, to hug. As we press into Jesus to embrace His matchless grace, the peace will return. The key for us to unlock His peace is to stop and seek the Lord.

Where do we search for Jesus? His Word. We must seek Him. *Seek* means "to go in search or quest of, to look for, to search for by going from place to place." I learned from Kay Smith that, in having devotions, you need to keep seeking, keep reading until you get a word that speaks to you. As I read my Bible and various devotionals, I keep reading until the Lord shows me something that brings His peace to my heart personally. Pursue Him and He will be found. His peace will surely follow.

"The righteous cry, and the Lord hears and delivers them out of all their troubles. The Lord is near to the brokenhearted and saves those who are crushed in spirit" (Ps. 34:17-18). You've heard the commercial say, "Dominos delivers;" but not like Jesus. He brings a word to the weary, hope to the downcast, comfort to those who are fearful. His delivery is 100% satisfaction guaranteed. He cannot fail. The trouble may seem insurmountable to you, but remember the Lord delivers!

So often as I write, I'm writing to myself. There

have been a few occasions when my peace was stolen and it unsettled me to my very core. The day the speech pathologist told me Grace Ann had Developmental Verbal Apraxia, I felt as if I'd received a blow to my stomach. My heart sank as I asked the hard question, "Would she ever mainstream? Would she ever catch up?" All the dreams I had for her were stolen and I felt like an 8.0 earthquake had just rocked my world. I sat at my kitchen counter and just sobbed like I was grieving a death. But as I digested the news and turned to the Lord, His peace captured my sadness and took control of my mind (Isa. 26:3).

"There is a future for the man of peace" (Ps. 37:37). "Great peace have they who love Your law, and nothing can make them stumble" (Ps. 119:165). May the God of all peace, grant peace to your borders (Ps. 147:14).

Perfect Peace, the Perfect Gift

Do not be anxious about anything,
but in everything, by prayer and petition,
with thanksgiving, present your requests to God.
And the peace of God, which transcends all
understanding, will guard your hearts
and your minds in Christ Jesus.
Philippians 4:6-7

Chapter 33

God's peace is surety for our soul. As we have seen through studying the fruit of the Spirit and desiring to be *fruitful in affliction*, it's all about relationship. Jesus is the key, first and foremost. He said, "These things I have spoken to you, that in Me you may have peace. In the world you will have tribulation; but be of good cheer, I have overcome the world" (John 16:33). For us to be fruitful and have peace in our hearts, we must keep Jesus as our focus. It is essential that we nurture our relationship with Him daily. It begins with worship. "Therefore, I urge you, brothers, in view of God's mercy, to offer your bodies as living sacrifices, holy and pleasing to God—this is your spiritual act of worship" (Rom. 12:1-2). As we take the time to adjust our minds on the Lord and simply worship Him, forgetting about ourselves, the peace of God will be ushered into our hearts. You will not find permanent peace in this world. It is only found in one place and one person, the Prince of Peace himself.

I love the promise found in Philippians 4:4-7. What are those things that steal your peace away? Is it a particular person in your life, unexpected bills, a recent job loss, a dying relative? The Lord desires to give us His peace instead of the anxiety that we are prone to feel. *Anxious* means "greatly concerned respecting something future or unknown; being in painful suspense." Anxiety is what "disturbs the mind, it expresses more than uneasiness or disturbance and even more than trouble or concern; it usually springs from fear or serious apprehension of evil." Perhaps our anxiety can be resolved by simply coming to the Lord and doing what the Word tells us to do: PRAY! Ask God for his guidance, thank Him for His many blessings. Present your requests to Him and see what He will do. As I have walked with the Lord these many years, He has not once ever failed me or let me down. He never ceases to amaze me in how He answers prayer. I believe the antidote for anxiousness is prayer, and the result is peace.

The peace God gives transcends all understanding; it rises above, surpasses, excels, goes beyond and passes over what I can comprehend. When my daughter was diagnosed with a severe speech issue it was devastating. But as I accepted it under the umbrella of God's sovereignty, I filtered it through my life verse: "For the Lord God is a sun and shield; the Lord will give grace and glory; no good thing will He withhold from those who walk uprightly" (Ps. 84:11). The peace came. I thought, "If God is allowing this—

and He is—then somehow it has to be good in His economy, otherwise He would withhold it." Amy Carmichael said, "In acceptance lieth peace." I always go back to that and it is such a comfort. The Lord truly gave me peace in a situation that, according to my understanding, should have rocked my world. Things would not change immediately or get better right away, and it meant she was going to need to work through this for some time. When her teachers told me she was behind and, with all their tests and reports, showed me how bad it really was on paper, the Lord gave me a peace that truly transcended my understanding and took my anxiety away. He has carried me in His peace all these years and I continue to trust that He is working it all for good, according to His Word. "Being confident of this very thing, that He who has begun a good work in you will complete it until the day of Jesus Christ" (Phil. 1:6).

This peace is not found in the world. It is so far beyond what the world offers. The peace of God is definitely out of this world! Ephesians 2:14 says, "For He himself is our peace." The peace is His to give. In the Amplified Bible John 14:27 says, "Peace I leave with you; My [own] peace I now give and bequeath to you. Not as the world gives do I give to you. Do not let your hearts be troubled, neither let them be afraid. [Stop allowing yourselves to be agitated and disturbed; and do not permit yourself to be fearful and intimidated and cowardly and unsettled.]" Peace belongs to Jesus, it is His property. He holds the pink slip (so to speak) on peace. The peace of the world is temporary and a fraud. It does not last and it's not the real deal. If Jesus is our peace, then all other attempts are simply a counterfeit. I love that peace is *His own* to give. He owns it completely; we could say He has a monopoly on peace! It's a gift as well as a byproduct, when we consider the fruit of the Spirit. When I am grounded in God's love and filled with his Spirit, His peace naturally springs forth in my life.

Another blessing of His peace is that it guards our hearts and minds. If you want to invest in the best security system for your mind, commit Isaiah 26:3 to memory. "You will keep him in perfect peace, whose mind is stayed on You, because he trusts in You." To *guard* is "to keep, protect, defend." God's peace is given to us to protect us from the assaults of the enemy. It is also "to secure against injury, loss or attack; to keep in safety." The enemy's mission is to rob, kill and destroy us—he will hurl insults and lies at us without even batting an eye. Thankfully God's peace secures our thoughts and keeps us safe from harm, mentally as well as physically. This is one of my favorite definitions: *guard* also means to accompany. Jesus is our lifeguard! He's with me every step of the way. "He walks with me and He talks with me and He tells me I am His own. And the joy we share as we tarry there, none other has ever known." Not only is there peace in knowing He is with me, but such joy as well. His eye is forever on me. *Guard* is a state of caution or vigilance. We guard our hearts and minds by being in the Word and seeking His counsel and direction. The Lord has many times given me *a peace* as a green light when I've been praying about a specific matter. Other times I've known in my spirit, I don't have a peace about this or that and the Lord has cautioned me to stand still and not take another step. He is the perfect crossing guard, giving His peace when it comes time to make decisions and cross the road. He's there to caution us from going down the wrong path. We simply need to acknowledge Him in all our ways and He will direct our paths. All His paths are peace.

"Let the peace of Christ rule in your hearts" (Col. 3:15). That word *rule* means to umpire in the Greek. Our English word *rule* means "that which is established as a principle, standard or directory; to govern; to control the will and actions of another." Synonyms for rule are influence, decide and reign. Umpires can certainly influence a game and they do decide calls. I pray that God's peace does indeed rule and reign in your heart. That it will have complete jurisdiction, command and sway over your thoughts, fears and any anxiety. We are not to be controlled by our emotions. May His peace influence your life so much so that it overrides, prevails and controls any anxious thought or care.

God's peace: *P*rotects our minds from anxiety, *E*ncourages our hearts, *A*ccompanies us always, *C*alms our fears, *E*mbraces us securely. What a blessing His peace is to our lives! It truly is perfect in every way.

"Now may the Lord of peace himself continually grant you peace in every circumstance" (2 Thess. 3:16).

The Merciful Patience of God

*The Lord is not slow in keeping His promise,
as some understand slowness. He is patient
with you, not wanting anyone to perish,
but everyone to come to repentance.*
2 Peter 3:9

Chapter 34

We can't talk about patience without looking at the life of Noah. He is an amazing example to us, revealing the patience of the Father. Patience has many ingredients, like the cranberry pumpkin spice muffins I made over Thanksgiving. Love is patient, it suffers long. It's not hasty, not over eager or impetuous; not easily provoked; not revengeful; but it's calm under injuries and offenses. It's persevering, calmly diligent; it is without discontent, without murmuring, without agitation and uneasiness. Galatians 5:22 in the Amplified Bible reads this way, "But the fruit of the [Holy] Spirit [the work which His presence within accomplishes] is love, joy (gladness), peace, patience (an even temper, forbearance)." Let's stop there. As we seek the Lord and desire to live fruitful lives, it will always be the Holy Spirit within us accomplishing this eternal work, not us. Remember it's the fruit *of* the Spirit.

In 2 Peter 3:9 we see where patience comes from:

the heart of God. It's shown in His love for souls. He is not willing that any should perish, but that all should come to repentance. In the Amplified translation, the word forbearance is alongside patience. *Forbearance* is "command of temper, restraint of passions, withholding from action, indulgence towards those who injure us, delay of resentment or punishment, not easily provoked." We need the Lord's forbearance when it comes to dealing with people. Beth Moore points out that this patience is inspired by mercy when it involves people.

I love the patience of God that is seen through the life of Noah. His story and testimony inspire and challenge me to live a fruitful life. In Genesis 6 I see five things of interest:

The Warning of God (v. 3)
The Wickedness of Man (v. 5)
The Walk of Noah (v. 8-9)
The Wonderful Plan of Salvation (v. 13-21)
The Worship Noah Offered to God (v. 22)

The Warning of God (Gen. 6:3). "My Spirit will not contend with man forever." We read in Genesis 6:1-2 there had been marriages of the sons of God with the daughters of men, perhaps intermarriage with the "godly line of Seth" to the "godless line of Cain." Man was growing more corrupt and living further from God. Thus the warning God issued. God's creation went from very good to very bad in just a short time. They started out in holiness and wholeness and sank to the whole of their imagination on evil.

The very people God had created to be fruitful and flourish became spoiled. Bad fruit has to be thrown out; when it's spoiled it's no good. To think God created man in His own image, in love, to enjoy fellowship with and bless. Man then became rebellious and rejected God. "The earth was depraved and putrid in God's sight, and the land was filled with violence (desecration, infringement, outrage, assault, and lust for power). And God looked upon the world and saw how degenerate, debased, and vicious it was, for all humanity had corrupted their way upon the earth and lost their true direction" (Gen. 6:11-12). It's no wonder the Lord wanted to start over.

The Wickedness of Man (Gen. 6:5). "The Lord saw how great man's wickedness on the earth had become, and that every inclination of the thoughts of his heart was only evil all the time." We are a truly wretched people apart from the grace of God. The Lord knows the thoughts and intents of our hearts and minds. I have a part-time cleaning job and the other day I was cleaning the inside door of the oven window. It was grimy, greasy and black. You couldn't see through the window at all. As I started scrubbing, the blackness became clear. It was slowly becoming clean. Some spots were stubborn and needed extra elbow grease to come clean, but the abrasive sponge I was using was accomplishing a miraculous feat. As I stared at the oven window, Genesis 6:5 came to my mind. Every inclination of their hearts was evil. Sin had taken over and their hearts were corrupt, stained, blackened. There was no cleanness in them at all, not a single spot of purity. When I saw that there was hope for this oven window, there was such joy in my heart. Victory was on its way. I was going to conquer this mess. Call me crazy, but I love cleaning. I love seeing dirty things become clean. And this oven window became such a portrait of God's grace and patience. It took some time to scrub it completely clean. When we come to Christ we are cleansed by the blood of Jesus immediately. "What can wash away my sin? Nothing but the blood of Jesus. What can make me whole again? Nothing but the blood of Jesus." Each day the Lord is scrubbing the spots of pride or fear away from our hearts and perfecting our faith. He's not into perfection like a person with OCD, so much as He's into purity. You see, when I finally got the oven window clean, I could see my reflection. The grease was gone, the blackness had vanished, the spots had disappeared and all that was left was my reflection. On that final day, when our sanctification is complete and we are fit for heaven, the Lord will see His reflection in us, just like the master goldsmith that heats up the gold to remove all the dross and scum. His plan is to purify the gold, bringing it to perfection in the process. The ultimate goal is for Him to be revealed. Sin hinders Him from being seen in our lives. But oh, the beauty that is revealed in a heart that has been washed by the blood of the Lamb!

The Walk of Noah (Gen. 6:8-9). I so admire and respect this man who chose to follow God in the midst of a crooked and perverse generation. He was a preacher of righteousness, finding grace in the eyes of God. In a time when sin abounded he walked

154

blameless with God. How important it is for us to have that daily fellowship with the Lord; to wake up in the morning with Him on our mind and to purpose to draw close to Him by being in His Word and prayer. The Lord certainly gave Noah forbearance for the work he was called to. He models a "command of temper, restraint of passions, withholding from action, delay of resentment or punishment, and being not easily provoked." I can't imagine what it was like for him, building the ark for 120 years while people were no doubt mocking him. May the Lord give us this patience with others that has command of our tempers when we are tempted to let loose.

The Wonderful Plan of Salvation (Gen. 6:13-21). God in His grace sought out Noah and provided a way for him and his family to be saved. "But I will establish My covenant (promise, pledge) with you, and you shall come into the ark—you and your sons and your wife and your sons' wives with you" (Gen. 6:18). Salvation is ALL OF GRACE! The Lord gave Noah a building project that lasted 120 years. All that time God was waiting for any and all who would repent. His wait was for just eight! The Lord showed his patience and forbearance with the people of the day, lovingly hoping they would turn from their wickedness. The Lord graciously delayed His punishment. He showed mercy towards those who were outright debase. His patience is profoundly limitless and unfailing. The heart that God had for his people became the heart of Noah. It's a good case of "like father, like son." "But God, who is rich in mercy, because of His great love with which He loved us, even when we were dead in trespasses, made us alive together with Christ (by grace you have been saved)" (Eph. 2:4-5). God's patience mingled with mercy offered salvation to a wicked, depraved, degenerate generation. He waited then and He waits today. He longs for those who are lost to come home. For the prodigals who have strayed, the backslidden and rebellious; he waits with open, loving arms. If you know someone who doesn't know the Lord, pray for them and with God's love and mercy share with them His wonderful plan of salvation. Who knows? They may be the one God is waiting for!

The Worship Noah Offered to God (Gen. 6:22). Noah is such an example to me in three aspects: he loved the Lord, loved those around him with the patience and forbearance of God, and he worshipped God in his obedience. "Noah did everything just as God commanded him" (Gen. 6:22). The Lord had given him a plan to follow for the construction of the ark and he obeyed the command. It's a good thing he did, too. Imagine if he had been slack or lazy or neglectful. The ark would not have been completed on time. I've heard obedience defined as the highest act of worship. A missionary friend of mine years ago told me my goal for teaching obedience to my children needs to be: instant, joyful and complete. (It's all a work in progress.) Noah obeyed ALL that the Lord instructed him to do. The Lord knew Noah's heart, that he could be entrusted with the task. He knew Noah would follow through.

May the Lord transform us by His Spirit into women who are filled with His loving patience, forbearing with those around us and having command of our tempers. May He help us to show mercy towards those who injure and easily provoke us. The order is certainly a tall one, but as we abide in Him we will be conformed to His loving, patient, merciful image. As daughters of the King, may we grow up to be like our heavenly Father: "The Lord, the Lord God, merciful and gracious, longsuffering, and abounding in goodness and truth" (Ex. 34:6). For then we will flourish with His fruitfulness!

"'Not by might nor by power, but by My Spirit,' says the Lord of Hosts" (Zech. 4:6).

Patience Rewarded

*Therefore do not cast away your confidence,
which has great reward. For you have need of
endurance, so that after you have done the will
of God, you may receive the promise.*
Hebrews 10:35-36

Chapter 35

Certainly there are circumstances in which each one of us is called to persevere. We are all in various stages of our lives. For some of us, we need to keep on going in homeschooling or maintain the course with our families. We all need to abide daily in Him, hold our ground and remain steadfast in our faith. We may not feel like we can be fruitful in affliction, but He who began a good work in you will complete it. It's not about us, but all about His amazing grace towards us. For someone perseverance may be physically pressing on in an illness and dealing with the scars that come with it. Perhaps there are emotional scars of the past, even spiritual scars that the Lord wants to heal us from. We are called to stand firm in our own course, knowing it's our precious Jesus who holds us together and sustains us. Jesus never wavered in His undying, unfailing love for us on the cross. Our Redeemer will without fail see us through to the finish line of our faith. He alone will carry us when we don't think we can make it through another day. Jesus will be faithful, come rain or shine, through thick and thin. Love never fails, because Jesus never fails.

"So do not throw away your confidence; it will be richly rewarded. You need to persevere so that when you have done the will of God, you will receive what he has promised" (Heb. 10:35-36). Perseverance is defined by Noah Webster as "persistence in anything undertaken; continued pursuit of any business or enterprise begun. In theology, continuance in a state of grace to a state of glory." That sounds like our entire life. As we walk in this world, we're going from strength to strength, covered by God's grace.

Just a few days ago, my mother-in-law passed away. She lived for 70 years, persevering in her faith and love for her Lord. Teresa ran her race and crossed the finish line into heaven. She was a godly wife, mother and grandmother. *Nagymama* (Hungarian for grandma) will be dearly missed by her family. She is enjoying the fruit of her labor, having done the will of God; she has received what He has promised (Heb. 10:36). What did God promise? A home in heaven! "In My Father's house are many mansions; if it were not so, I would have told you. I go to prepare a place for you" (John 14:2). Teresa has a beautiful mansion in heaven with her beloved Savior and is now reunited with her husband of 36 years. Together they raised their children to know and love the Lord, leaving behind a godly heritage. They took their job seriously, and did it well as unto the Lord. What more is there for a parent to do?

As we continue on in this life, Jesus is our daily pursuit. Knowing Him and making Him known is our desire. "To those who by perseverance in doing good seek for glory and honor and immortality, eternal life" (Rom. 2:7). That's us! This world is not our home. We are told that where our treasure is, that is where our hearts will be. Some of us have treasures in heaven, those whom we love and miss dearly. We do not sorrow as those who have no hope; we have a living hope because Jesus is our risen Savior who conquered the grave. One day we will be reunited with those loved ones, and what a truly glorious day it will be. Oh, happy day . . . I can hardly wait!

Synonyms for *perseverance* are "continuance, persistence, keep on, hold on, abide, pursue, stick to, maintain its course, endure, carry on, sustain, uphold, unvaried, undying, steadiness, grit, stamina, backbone, tenacity, staying power, steadfast, unwavering, without fail, through thick and thin, rain or shine."

One of my favorite coffee cups has the best definition of *mother* I've ever read, and I'm sure you will love it too. It reminds me of my mother and mother-in-law and their persevering love. "Mother: a female parent known to be able to hold dinner, hold a job, hold down the fort, hold a hand, and hold on to her pocketbook all at the same time. One who can keep a secret, keep her cool, keep a promise, keep a house, keep the faith, and through it all keep smiling. Someone who gives support, gives a hand, gives good advice, gives her word, gives her time and gives love to her family everyday of her life." Our lives are all about holding on to the hope of Jesus, keeping the faith and giving our all for Him so that one day we too will hear, "Well done good and faithful servant," from our beloved bridegroom.

"And not only this, but we also exult in our tribulations, knowing that tribulation brings about perseverance" (Rom. 5:3). The Lord is in the business of construction, building our character everyday by the trials He allows in our lives. There is a plan and purpose in our sorrow that is working for good and ultimately bringing forth the fruitfulness He desires in our lives. "For I know the thoughts that I think toward you, says the Lord, thoughts of peace and not of evil, to give you a future and a hope" (Jer. 29:11).

"Many are the afflictions of the righteous, but the Lord delivers him out of them all" (Ps. 34:19). My mom had cancer many years ago and I prayed for the Lord to heal her. Her deliverance finally came when Jesus took her home nearly 18 years ago. The Lord healed her and made her whole differently than I wanted, but His ways are just and true. My mother-in-law suffered a stroke just a little over a month ago, leaving her paralyzed and eventually leading to her passing. I can rest in God's sovereignty and love for me when afflictions come because there is much fruit borne out of sorrow.

Jesus made it so simple for us. He condensed the whole law into two commands: love God and love your neighbor. We know we're to be in fellowship with other believers, to attend church and pray; but persevering day to day, moment by moment is where the rubber meets the road. It is a conscious choice we make when the grief hits, when the waves of doubt crash upon us or fear strikes our hearts. We are to trust in the Lord, to believe His promise, rejoice in faith and hopefully say, "It is well, oh my soul." In those moments, victory is won, the enemy silenced; and our Father looks down with no greater joy than to see that his children walk in truth. "The Lord your God in your midst, the Mighty One, will save; He will rejoice over you with gladness, He will quiet you with His love, He will rejoice over you with singing" (Zeph. 3:17).

"Therefore, we ourselves speak proudly of you among the churches of God for your perseverance and faith in the midst of all your persecutions and afflictions which you endure" (2 Thess. 1:4). May it be true of us as well; that we too, having persevered in our afflictions, will have kept the faith and borne much fruit, knowing one day it will all be rewarded in heaven.

Yet Will I Hope in Him

Though He slay me, yet will I trust Him.
Even so, I will defend my own ways before Him.
Job 13:15

Chapter 36

We recently learned about Job's perseverance in the midst of his trials. He becomes an example for us as one who seeks and pursues the Lord. The *patience of Job* is a phrase that we attribute to those who have an unparalleled measure of patience. Even though Job suffered trial upon trial he was able to say, "Though He slay me, yet will I hope in Him" (Job 13:15). At the core of his patience was a hope that did not disappoint or waver. It really comes down to a choice we make each day. Will we choose to place our hope in the person of Jesus Christ who does not fail, or will we lose hope altogether? Job chose to hope in God regardless of his circumstances. Somehow he knew in faith the principle of Romans 8:28 that "all things work together for good to those who love God, to those who are the called according to His purpose."

Job's faith was clearly tested for he says in Job 23:10, "But He knows the way that I take; when He has tested me, I shall come forth as gold." In this world we will have tribulation. There seems to be more suffering in this world as the days go by. But our hope and peace are to be in God. And this hope is directly linked to the filling of the Holy Spirit. It's like an ice cube tray that is filled up at one end; inevitably the empty spaces along the way overflow as well as they are under the flow of water. In the same way the Spirit fills our hearts with the love of God which affects our hope and peace. "The fruit of the Spirit is love, joy, peace, patience . . ." (Gal. 5:22). The more of Him that there is in my life, the more of his love is evidenced. And so the progression leads to more joy as we go through the trials, and more patience as we deal with challenging situations and people. It is vital that we sit at Jesus' feet so that we hear His Word and find our hope in Him.

Having hope in the Lord enables us to stand where God has us and hinge our future on God Himself. "[What, what would have become of me] had I not believed that I would see the Lord's goodness in the land of the living! Wait and hope for and expect the Lord; be brave and of good courage and let your heart be stout and enduring. Yes, wait for and hope for and expect the Lord" (Ps. 27:13-14). The psalmist writes, "My hope is in you" (Ps. 25:5). The author of Psalm 119 continually says, "I hope in Your word" (v. 81). One of my very favorite verses is, "For I know the thoughts that I think toward you, says the Lord, thoughts of peace and not of evil, to give you a future and a HOPE" (Jer. 29:11).

The hope Job reveals speaks to me about: a person, a promise, power, purpose, priority and a bigger picture!

The person on which we base our hope is Jesus

Christ, my precious Savior. HE is our living hope (1 Pet. 1:3). We've been singing that worship song at church lately: "Christ is risen from the dead, we are one with Him again, come awake . . . Christ is risen from the dead, trampling over death by death, come awake . . . Come and rise up from the grave!" We have a risen Savior! Without that we would have no hope.

The promise of hope comes from His Word. 1 Corinthians 1:9 says, "God is faithful, by whom you were called into the fellowship of His Son, Jesus Christ our Lord." This promise offers me great hope for my daughter who also is called by God. The entire book of Psalms is there with encouragement of His hope.

His power gives me hope because I know He is able to do exceedingly abundantly above all I ask or think (Eph. 3:20). His power is made available to us through His Holy Spirit (Acts 1:8). There is power in prayer as we come together to pray for one another. Where two or more are gathered in His name to pray, He is there in the midst of them (Matt. 18:20).

His purpose is made clear to me when I'm in His Word and listening to His voice. This in turn sets our priorities in order giving us hope that, when we purpose in our hearts to serve Him and stay loyal to Him like Job, we too will find favor with Him and have hope for our future.

The Lord has a bigger picture for us to live out. Some of you are wives and mothers, but we're also His daughters placed within the body of Christ. He wants to use you to touch and encourage someone else as they go through trials. Everything that you have gone through and are presently going through can be used by the Lord to minister to someone else. You can offer them the hope you have in the Lord, testifying of His faithfulness to carry you through the tough times.

It is this very hope in the Lord, that He is able to take a misery and turn it into a ministry, which brought about and birthed Hope Outreach Ministry— a ministry with the vision of reaching out to moms with special needs children. If you have a friend with a special needs child or are the mom of a special needs child, contact Hope Outreach Ministry at hopeoutreachirvine@yahoo.com or check out the Facebook page for more information. Offer yourself to Him. "Hope in God, for I shall again praise Him for the help of His presence" (Ps. 42:5). May your faith be like Job's so you too can say, "Though He slay me, yet will I hope in Him" (Job 13:15).

With Patience Comes Hope

Remember Your word to Your servant,
for You have given me hope.
Psalm 119:49

Chapter 37

What must we do to be fruitful in the arena of patience? The answer is simpler that you probably think: we just abide in Jesus. He will do the work in us. We just need to fix our eyes on Him, the author and finisher of our faith and hang in there. Peaches don't work hard at being a peach, they just abide in the branch and in time they are ripe for the picking. Jesus is our branch, and we must stay connected to Him if we desire the fruit to come in our lives. Have you ever prayed for patience? It's the quickest way to enter into a trial that will test your patience! Some trials are for the long haul. This is where we need endurance. It is a key component of patience which speaks of permanence, stability and continuance. "Remember Your word to Your servant, for You have given me hope" (Ps. 119:49).

As God is growing patience in us, He desires to develop our character as well. Hope and endurance are integral components of patience. Like a soldier in boot camp that needs to endure and maintain his course, we too must run our race with endurance. My friend's son just graduated from boot camp and is now proudly serving as a Marine reservist. He persevered through many hardships. One particular challenge was a fractured bone in his leg which the doctor had told him was a stress fracture. It ended up being 90% fractured. He exemplified such tenacity and backbone to persist and carry on to the end of boot camp and finish. I'm sure it wasn't easy—in fact I know it wasn't—but he remained steadfast and unwavering, even when he could of quit. He chose to stick to it and finish his course. His example of perseverance is what patience with hope is all about.

How do patience and hope work together? What is *hope*? It is "that which furnishes ground of expectation or promises desired good." Our hope is found in HIM—it goes back to a person. I need the hope of heaven to carry me though the day. "For the Lord himself will descend from heaven with a shout, with the voice of an archangel, and with the trumpet of God. And the dead in Christ will rise first. Then we who are alive and remain shall be caught up together with them in the clouds to meet the Lord in the air. And thus we shall always be with the Lord. Therefore comfort one another with these words" (I Thess. 4:16-18).

I need God's hope that He will see me though my trials and I expect Him to fulfill His promise that He who has begun a good work will complete it (Phil. 1:6). I bank on it every day. Thankfully we are not a people who have no hope (1 Cor. 15:12-19).

I love acrostics—they are a fun little way to ponder God's Word: HOPE.

H—Heaven is near. This world is not our home.

O—Open your eyes and look up. Ask the Lord to give you His perspective.

P—Pray with someone and press on.

E—Expect the Lord to do exceedingly abundantly above all you ask or think. Expect Him to come to your rescue when you call. Remember eternity is on the horizon. There will be a day coming soon when everything will be made right. Hold on to the hope of heaven.

Ask the Lord to give you a promise, a word that gives you hope. Then pray it, cling to it and cash it in to the Lord each day. "Remember your word to your servant, for you have given me hope" (Ps. 119:49). Thank Him for His promise. Praise Him that He will fulfill it in His way and in His timing. Wait for Him to complete that work and, in the meantime, continue to serve Him. Wait doesn't mean we do nothing and sit idly. *Wait* means to wait on, like a waiter at a restaurant; you serve Him. It can be by just sitting at His feet when you have devotions or at work as you faithfully and diligently do your best unto Him and for His glory.

Patiently Persevering, Part 1

He knows the way that I take;
when He has tested me, I will come forth as gold.
Job 23:10

Chapter 38

I love acrostics, as you well know by now. This is what the Lord showed me about perseverance, which is linked to being patient.

P—There's a *person* who is always with us as we are called to persevere in our lives: Jesus. "For He himself has said, 'I will never desert you, nor will I ever forsake you'" (Heb. 13:5). He is by your side, leading and guiding you each step of the way. His peace comforts your heart. His promises give you hope. His presence enables us to hang in there, maintain our course, press on and not lose our faith.

E—There's an *eternal* plan at work in our lives as we travel on heavenward. God does work all things together for good to those who love God, to those who are called according to His purpose (Rom. 8:28). This is our hope that, no matter what comes our way, God will bring good out of it. He is especially at work in our lives in the midst of the pain we bear, in our grief. 2 Corinthians 4:17 says, "For momentary, light affliction is producing for us an eternal weight of glory far beyond all comparison." There is an eternal benefit to all that God allows in our lives.

R—*Resting* in Him. Psalm 37:7 says, "Rest in the Lord and wait patiently for Him." *Rest* is "cessation of motion or action of any kind, quiet, a state of reconciliation to God." "Learn of Me; for I am meek and lowly in heart: and you shall find rest to your souls" (Matt. 11:29). *Rest* is "to acquiesce; as to rest on heaven's determination, to continue fixed; we rest our cause on the truth of the Scripture." The world is restless, uneasy, unquiet and unsettled. As Christians we rest in Jehovah Jireh, the provider of all we have needed. He provided a ram when Abraham needed a sacrifice. He became the last lamb the world would ever need. He gives us rest; quietness to our soul and peace to trust Him in our deepest sorrows. He is in control and on the throne; at work behind the scenes of our lives. We don't have to strive, plot or plan. "The Lord will accomplish what concerns me" (Ps. 138:8). Picture a baby at perfect rest in his mother's arms: at total rest, perfect peace, no cares, no worries, no stress. Oh, how He longs to take His kids up in His arms and hold them close, shielding them from all fear, that they might receive His rest.

S—*Stand* firm. To *stand* is "to be fixed or steady, not to vacillate, to hold a course, to have direction; to adhere to; to abide, to be permanent; to endure; to maintain." We are in a marathon, not a sprint. Some of you have persevered for years in prayer, waiting for that loved one to come to Jesus. During this marathon we're to grow and know the shepherd of our soul. He's the Good Shepherd (John 10:11), the Great Shepherd (Heb. 13:20-21) and the Chief

Shepherd (1 Peter 5:4). Shepherds have one concern: their sheep. They will do anything to protect, feed, nurture and care for their beloved little lambs. Our Shepherd loved us to death. He cared for you so much, He stooped down and became the lamb who was slain for the sins of the world. Draw near to Him and He will draw near to you. Knowing Him is the greatest joy. He will strengthen you and cause you to press on, being steadfast, immovable, standing on the promises of God.

E—Evidence of His power, peace and presence upon us. When Moses came down from the mountain it was obvious that he had been with God; it was all over his face. As we are called to keep going, to press on, not giving up or giving in, we know the Shepherd of our soul will support us along the way. God will give us opportunities to share and testify of His goodness and faithfulness, proclaiming what He has done on our behalf. The world is searching for answers, but they don't know it's really Jesus they need. We are those living sermons for them to read, revealing God's handiwork. As we are humbled and reduced to nothing, we can share that it is the Lord who has done it all. He's comforted us in our mourning, carried us through the fiery trial and given us hope when we felt we had no hope.

(It might require some *perseverance* to finish this very long word in one sitting, so we will continue in the next chapter. Until then, blessings, dear sister.)

Patiently Persevering, Part 2

He knows the way that I take;
when He has tested me, I will come forth as gold.
Job 23:10

Chapter 39

V—Victory in the midst of persevering. We overcome by the blood of the Lamb and the word of His testimony. Remember Joseph, he certainly persevered. He didn't throw a pity party when he was literally thrown in a pit by his brothers. He was silent like Jesus. Joseph chose to forgive like Jesus. "This is the victory that has overcome the world, even our faith" (1 John 5:4). It's by faith in Him. Romans 8:37 says, "But in all these things we overwhelmingly conquer through Him who loved us." Remember Paul & Silas praising God in the prison. Victory doesn't mean the end or the completion of the trial but *in the middle of it*, when I'm tempted to throw in the towel or give in to the lies of the enemy. Instead of doing those things I, like Paul, praise and worship God in faith regardless of my circumstances and sing, "Blessed be Your name, on the road marked with suffering. Though there's pain in the offering, blessed be Your name." Only Jesus gives us victory over cancer, the death of a loved one, a prodigal and a child's disability because He alone lifts our eyes to heaven.

Jehoshaphat prayed in 2 Chronicles 20:12, "For we are powerless before this great multitude who are coming against us; nor do we know what to do, but our eyes are on You." That's victory! Psalm 141:8 declares "For my eyes are toward You, O God, the Lord; in You I take refuge." He makes us soar in the heavenlies where we can live above the trial; not crushed underneath it in despair and hopeless, but full of confidence in Him who is our living hope: the King of Kings and Lord of Lords. In Him we have victory over sin, the enemy, the grave. Praise be to Jesus who said in John 16:33, "These things I have spoken to you, so that in Me you may have peace. In the world you have tribulation, but take courage; I have overcome the world."

E—Endurance. The Lord is building our endurance from one trial to the next; love endures all things. We know Jesus loves us, as He proved it on the cross. With that truth we can press on, knowing whatever comes our way, this too shall pass. There's a blessing for those who endure. James 5:11 says, "We count those blessed who endured. You have heard of the endurance of Job and have seen the outcome of the Lord's dealings, that the Lord is full of compassion and is merciful." Job knew His redeemer lived! And somehow he knew that one day His redeemer would come and stand upon the earth. This is our hope too. Beth Moore said, "In Scripture we hold in our hands vast promises that Job never held, assuring us that God will work our pain toward perfection." I love that. The Lord is building us up in our most holy faith through every pain. Our trust and faith increase as we

174

grow and persevere, as well as the fruit He desires to bring forth in our lives. We endure like the runner who has one goal: to cross the finish line. We, too, run this race to win. Paul said in Philippians 3:12 & 14, "I press on so that I may lay hold of that for which also I was laid hold of by Christ Jesus. . . . I press on toward the goal for the prize of the upward call of God in Christ Jesus." Our finish line is heaven and one day soon we shall cross it and see Jesus on the other side. It will ALL be worth it—every tear, every pang in our heart, every prayer prayed in faith, every opportunity we have had to trust in Him.

R—*Reward.* Our reward will certainly be in heaven, and even now we are told to lay up treasures there. Hebrews 11:26 speaks of Moses "esteeming the reproach of Christ greater riches than the treasures in Egypt; for he looked to the reward." What was the reward Moses sought after? I believe it was seeing his deliverer and Messiah face to face. We will be rewarded with crowns that we will gladly lay at Jesus' feet. Another reward will be answered prayer, being in heaven and seeing how God worked and answered our petitions, the cries of our heart.

May the Lord strengthen you this day to press on in patience with the people around you and the situations you face.

Patiently Persevering, Part 3

He knows the way that I take;
when He has tested me, I will come forth as gold.
Job 23:10

Chapter 40

A—Acknowledging Him. It was extremely simple and yet so incredibly profound: the testimony of a mother who said, "I will rejoice," while still grieving the death of her son; it spoke volumes to me. Her three words revealed her heart, choosing to praise God in the midst of unimaginable sorrow. I will rejoice. I will still trust even if God takes them home, even if . . . (you fill in the blank). For me it was hearing that my daughter had an extremely severe speech problem. For years she was virtually silent, but by God's amazing grace she has made incredible progress and is now speaking in sentences. Not perfect ones, but that's okay! He who has begun a good work in her will be faithful to complete it. She also has an auditory processing disorder, where she has a hard time remembering bits of sequential information. Even in this I am challenged to still praise and trust Him in faith, acknowledging that He is good and knows best (Prov. 3:5-6). He is an anchor for my soul.

N—Knowing Him (it really should begin with an

N). "For I know whom I have believed and am persuaded that He is able to keep what I have committed to Him until that day" (2 Tim. 1:12). Know your God. Know His character. Know that He is loving and gracious, kind and compassionate. He is near to the brokenhearted. He is wonderful beyond words. He is incredibly forgiving and patient; this I know. His mercy is higher than the heavens and His faithfulness is deeper than the sea. Know that you know Jesus is on your side. Know that He loves you. Job said, "For I know that my Redeemer lives" (Job 19:25). Know that nothing can separate you from the Love of God (Rom. 8:35-39). Know His Word and precious promises. Mark them in your Bible and date them as stones of remembrance. Know He is good. I have this habit of marking crowns in my Bible every time I come to the character of God. When I spot a crown, I'm reminded of His character. Here are just a few I found going through the Psalms: He is mighty, maker of heaven and earth, my helper, Lord Jehovah, gracious, great in mercy, my keeper, my shade, my protector, my guard, my deliverer, the stiller of every storm, the sustainer of my soul, my refuge and present help in time of need, my Savior! Begin your own list today, you will know Him more and be on the road to bearing fruit.

C—*Continue* each day in His Word. The Lord Jesus made it so simple for us to follow Him. There are only two commandments we need to keep: love God and love people. That essentially sums up our Christian faith. It's putting it into practice that trips us up. How do we show our love for Jesus? He said, "If you continue in My Word, then you are truly disciples of Mine" (John 8:31). My favorite part of the day is waking up early before the kids, sitting with Jesus, my Bible and coffee, and hearing His sweet voice. His Word is the lamp unto our feet and the light unto our path. For us to live fruitful lives, we must be in His Word. It is there we discover His will for our lives, find comfort, peace, wisdom, instruction and direction. I can't imagine living a day without His Word that communicates His heart to my life. Just last night in our Wednesday night Bible study, my pastor was teaching in 1 Kings 22 where Jehoshaphat made an alliance with King Ahab—a bad decision. He had previously sought the Lord in 2 Chronicles 17, positioning himself against Ahab. He followed the God of his fathers and did not act as Israel did; he had the law of the Lord taught in Judah. At one time he was devoted to the Lord, took delight in the Lord and frequently came before the Lord. But somewhere along the way, he allied himself by marriage with Ahab (2 Chron. 18:1). He entered into a relationship where he was unequally yoked with an evil king. His discernment became foggy, as my pastor said, and it led to compromise. We desperately need spiritual discernment and it only comes from continuing daily in the Word. Bank employees spend countless hours handling real money. As soon as a counterfeit comes their way they know because it feels differently. And even though it is off ever so slightly, they discern it immediately. When we are in the Word, continuing in the faith, we hear the voice of our Shepherd. His voice becomes recognizable to our hearts. May you continue in the grace of God (Acts 13:43). I encourage you, "Continue in the faith, firmly established and steadfast, and not moved away from the hope of the gospel that you have heard" (Col. 1:23). And most of all, "Let brotherly love continue" (Heb. 13:1).

E—Expect with hope that the Lord will do great and mighty things. "We continually remember before our God and Father your work produced by faith, your labor prompted by love, and your endurance inspired by hope in our Lord Jesus Christ" (1 Thess. 1:3). Hope is a key element of patience, which is linked to perseverance and endurance. Beth Moore explains, "The Greek word for hope is *elpis*, and it means the desire of some good with the expectation of obtaining it." When my mom passed away, I came home from the hospital and asked the Lord to give me some hope for my hurting heart. It was April 23rd and I could hardly think where to turn in my Bible. He lovingly brought me to Proverbs 23:18, "For surely there is a hereafter, and your hope will not be cut off." Missing my mom, I needed hope that one day I'd see her again in heaven. I truly expect to see her along with my in-laws and all those who have gone on before. I love Jeremiah 29:11; it is a constant source of hope and comfort. The King James Version reads, "For I know the thoughts that I think toward you, saith the Lord, thoughts of peace, and not of evil, to give you an expected end." The New International Version reads, "'For I know the plans I have for you,' declares the Lord, 'plans to prosper you and not to harm you, plans to give you hope and a future.'" God has our future in His hands. This we can confidently hope in. Heaven is real. As Proverbs 23:18 says, there surely is a hereafter. This world is not all there is. That alone is reason to hope! If this life is not the end and the Lord has a bigger plan— one of peace and not of evil—I can walk in victory, expecting Him to bring fruit from every affliction. I expect Him to bring some good from my heartaches; not because I deserve it, but because He promised it to His children who love Him! The good work He is doing is transforming us to be more like Jesus: more of Him and less of ourselves, more of His love in our lives, more compassion for others who are hurting, a quicker urgency to pray for friends when they ask, the ability to forgive as Christ did, remembering He forgave us when we were yet sinners. Expect the Lord to come through for you. Expect Him to be there in the morning when you come to sit at His feet. Expect Him to answer your prayers, even if the answer is "no" or "wait" or "not yet, but in My timing." We have a living hope! "Blessed be the God and Father of our Lord Jesus Christ, who according to His abundant mercy has begotten us again to a living hope through the resurrection of Jesus Christ from the dead" (1 Peter 1:3).

In conclusion, there's a *person* with us as we are called to persevere in our lives. There's an *eternal* plan at work as we travel on heavenward. We are to *rest* in Him and *stand* firm in the faith. There will be *evidence* of His power, peace and presence upon us to those around us. He gives us the *victory* when we abide in Him. *Endurance* comes from Him to run this race. He is our *reward* as we keep our eyes on the prize. *Acknowledge* Him, even in your deepest sorrow, and He will be faithful to order your steps. *Knowing* Him is our greatest joy on earth, make Him known! *Continue* each day in His Word. *Expect* with hope that the Lord will do great and mighty things, to Him be all the glory.

It had never dawned on me, before I received a particular email, the blessing Grace Ann had given me. As Hope Outreach Ministry began to unfold, a new mom came to one of our gatherings. Just two days later, she and her twelve-year-old son were in the ER. He had fallen and broken his wrist in two places. One of the hardest things to deal with, as a mother of a child with special needs, is having to explain to everyone the issues your child faces. An email was sent out to all the moms to pray. I prayed for the Lord's peace to comfort my friend and her son. The next morning she wrote of miracle after miracle that the Lord had done for her in answering prayer. God is so good. It amazed me to read that she was thankful for a group of ladies that she could call on to pray for her son. In all her years of raising her son with special needs, she had never had a group of moms to go to for prayer. It hit me that if it wasn't for Grace Ann I wouldn't be in this place to pray for another mom and see the Lord bring his peace to one who really needed it. After ten long years I was beginning to see that the Lord had a plan all along. I just needed to persevere and keep my hope in Him.

The Kindness of the King

David asked, "Is there anyone
still left of the house of Saul to whom I can show
kindness for Jonathan's sake?"
2 Samuel 9:1

Chapter 41

One of my all-time favorite chapters in the Bible is 2 Samuel 9. It's the story of King David and Mephibosheth, Jonathan's son. Within this portion of Scripture is a beautiful portrait of our King's kindness towards us, his children.

The fruit of the Spirit is love. That love is revealed to us through the kindness in His heart. We in turn are told to, "Be kind to one another, tenderhearted" (Eph. 4:32). We will surely see the tender heart of the King in these verses. First we will look at the chapter from the perspective of the King. Then we will view the response of Mephibosheth. Please read 2 Samuel 9:1-12, it is short yet powerful.

First, notice in 2 Samuel 9:1 that *the King sought out Mephibosheth*: "David asked, 'Is there anyone still left of the house of Saul to whom I can show kindness for Jonathan's sake?'" Within the heart of King David was a well of kindness, a reservoir of love that needed to be drawn upon. Our heavenly Father loves us immensely, beyond our comprehension. God is love. Not a day goes by that He doesn't think of His children and long to lavish them with His loving kindness. Remember how Jesus wept looking over Jerusalem. He longed to gather the people into His loving arms but they were not willing to come to Him. It is the Lord's kindness that has drawn us unto Him. Be on the lookout for His kindness as you hear His still, small voice speaking over you. He may reveal His kindness through answered prayer or through a friend who does some act of kindness for you.

Secondly, upon discovering that there was a living relative of Jonathan's, the king asked, "Where is He?" (2 Sam. 9:4). David wanted to find him for one purpose. Our King had a purpose in His heart too; it was for our salvation. It's His kindness that led us to repentance. Maybe you know the song, "Knowing that You love us, no matter what we do, makes us want to love You too. If You are for us, who can be against us? You gave us everything, even Your only Son." Our King not only found us and saved us, but He gave us everything He had: His Son. What kindness! Our King knows where we are at any given moment. He knows our name. He has our address. He sees our lives, our hardships and our heartaches. He knows every tear that falls. Take comfort—your King knows where you're at emotionally, physically and financially. He knows the grieving heart of the one who just buried her mother. He knows the sorrow and the pain of the mother who has a special needs child. He knows those who have lost their jobs and are hurting financially. Not only does He know, but He will show forth His kindness. He will provide the means that we need. He will give us strength for the *day*, not a week or month or a year at a time. Our King cannot fail. For all of history (which really is *His story*), He's been leading and guiding His people. Will you be the exception and His first failure? I don't think so. Our King has a wealth of resources. There are unlimited storehouses of love and grace, goodness and mercy, kindness and peace that He is just waiting to give out.

Thirdly, 2 Samuel 9:5 says, "So King David had him brought from Lo Debar." I like the King James Version, "Then King David sent, and fetched him." Our precious King Jesus was sent from His Father to die for our sins. The servant of the king knew where Mephibosheth was living. The orders were given to bring him back to the king. By God's grace and loving kindness we've been drawn unto Him by the Holy Spirit. We've been drawn with His cords of love (Hosea 11:4). David wrote in Psalm 40 that God had saved him from a horrible pit and drew him out of the miry clay. We've all been in places where we felt like we were in a pit. David had experienced firsthand the deliverance of God. He had cried out to the Lord in his distress and the Lord rescued him. Our King has fetched us out of the miry clay of sin, out of a horrible pit, and set our feet upon the rock. He also bids us to come to Him.

Fourth, we see David's response when Mephibosheth arrives. I'm sure it was with love and grace in his eyes, "'Don't be afraid,' David said to him, 'for I will surely show you kindness for the sake

of your father Jonathan. I will restore to you all the
land that belonged to your grandfather Saul, and you
will always eat at my table" (2 Sam. 9:7). Did you
notice all those *I wills*? The King's word is a sure thing,
a done deal.

Wow, have you ever seen such love? It just welled
up within King David. Maybe that's why David was
called a *man after God's own heart*, because he
showed forth the heart of God. There are three things
to take note of in David's response. First, His words
were gracious, promising and comforting. That's our
King too. He quiets our fears with just a word.
Secondly, David said, "For Jonathan's sake." Our
heavenly Father shows us His kindness because of
Jesus' sake and sacrifice on the cross. Third, the king
gave his promise and that *settled* the issue of fear for
Mephibosheth. It *secured* his future. And it *silenced* all
his doubts.

Our King reassures us daily with promises to fear
not. "For I am the Lord, your God, who takes hold of
your right hand and says to you, 'Do not fear; I will
help you'" (Isa. 41:13). "Fear not, for I have
redeemed you. . . . When you pass through the
waters, I will be with you" (Isa. 43:1-2). "In
righteousness you will be established: Tyranny will be
far from you; you will have nothing to fear" (Isa.
54:14). His "perfect love drives out fear (1 John 4:18).
Don't you know your King has perfect love toward
you? May His kindness settle the issue of fear, bring
security to your heart that He has your future and
silence all your doubts!

The king promised to restore the land that was his

by right. He was going to reinstate that which was his rightful inheritance. We have no inheritance to claim by right, we deserve hell; but our King's kindness continues on into eternity where He graciously has set up a layaway inheritance plan for us. As we lay up treasures in heaven, our inheritance is being added to daily. It's a better plan than any retirement pension or 401k you'll ever get here on earth!

Lastly, Mephibosheth was given a place to always eat at the king's table. What provision, what love, what kindness the king extended to him. Our King restores the years that the locusts have eaten (Joel 2:25). He takes us from a barren wilderness and sits us at His banqueting table of love to feast on His goodness. May you, this day, bask in the kindness of your King Jesus. Receive by faith all He has for you: gracious words, precious promises, restoration, liberation and a secure future. There's a table awaiting you. May you come and dine with Him daily, enjoying the communion and fellowship of your King. Once you've tasted His goodness you'll never be satisfied at any other table. As you have freely received, may you freely give. That's living a fruitful life!

Appropriating His Promises

But when the kindness and love of God
our Savior appeared, He saved us, not because
of righteous things we had done,
but because of His mercy.
Titus 3:4

Chapter 42

In the last chapter, we viewed 2 Samuel 9 focusing on the kindness of the king. The heart of this chapter will be *appropriating His promises*. It's one thing to have the promises of God in our Bibles and read them, but it's quite another to take them into our hearts and make them our own. There are valuable lessons to learn from the life of Mephibosheth: his example in going before the king, stepping out in faith, acting on the word of the King and finally claiming his possession. Applying God's truths to our lives brings a fragrant fruitfulness!

Remember Mephibosheth lived in a barren, desolate place called Lo Debar. He was pasture-less. This was no dream vacation spot. It was definitely a place of obscurity where he just merely existed, and most likely it was a depressing place. In those days when a new king seized the throne it was the practice to wipe out all existing family members of the former king. David's best friend Jonathan was the rightful heir to his father Saul's throne. But Jonathan willingly laid aside his right to the throne, knowing God had called David to be king.

Fifteen years pass and David has a thought, "I wonder if Jonathan has any relatives still living?" He didn't want to do him in, He wanted to do him some good! All the while Mephibosheth was living, hiding out, keeping a low profile. He had suffered the loss of his father and grandfather in battle, all at the age of five. Another trial he faced was the fact that he was crippled. He had suffered a fall when his nanny dropped him (2 Sam. 4:4). She had heard about the battle and the death of King Saul and, fearing for the life of Little M (he needs a nickname), she was running with him trying to escape. Tragically, he became lame in both feet. Now if that's not enough, his name—and a long one at that—means "shameful breath." Some suggest it could have been an asthma-related issue. This man had lived the majority of his life in affliction, heartache, sorrow upon sorrow, possibly in depression. But that's all about to change. Just wait and see.

What about you? Has it been a tough week, a tough month, a tough year? What has crippled you? What disability is plaguing you or a loved one? Do you feel inept, incomplete, incapable, helpless and perhaps even hopeless? Is depression an issue you struggle with? Are you crippled with the fear of failure? We may feel all these things: unqualified, disabled, good for nothing, inadequate. And in reality, we are powerless to do anything apart from God. We are just like Mephibosheth: lame, plain and simple. But there is good news for us and for Little M too! The king is calling and his servant is on the way to fetch Mephibosheth.

Here is our first example to follow from this precious man Mephibosheth, found in 2 Samuel 9:6, "When Mephibosheth son of Jonathan, the son of Saul, came to David, *he bowed down to pay him honor*." He came to the king in humility and paid him honor. He acknowledged the king's throne and worthiness. We too are to come before our King humbly in full surrender, seeking to find grace in His eyes. And that's exactly what Mephibosheth found, a heart overflowing with kindness and goodness that couldn't help but show it forth in a tangible way. Perhaps there was still a lingering fear or doubt with Mephibosheth. He didn't know why the king had summoned him. But he stepped out in faith and came to him regardless of his feelings. He didn't let his handicap hold him back.

It was the heart of the king that wanted to do him some good! We saw the overwhelming display of the king's kindness and his promises to restore Mephibosheth. In verse 8 he bows again, recognizing his condition when he says, "What is your servant, that you should notice a dead dog like me?" Lesson number two: It's in the presence of the King that we truly see ourselves for who we really are. God is holy and we are not. The King is all glorious and at His feet we realize we are nothing. King David has just made Mephibosheth the offer of a lifetime. His *condition* is the same: he's still lame; but his *position* has changed for good. (For eternity and for the better.) We are saved by God's amazing grace. Before coming to Christ we were lame and wretched sinners. But in Christ, we're a new creation, old things are passed away and behold all things are made new. We are *in Him*. We still have a sin nature to contend with, but we're robed in Christ's righteousness and washed in His blood. When the Father sees me, He sees me positionally in Christ, holy and blameless.

The chapter closes with Mephibosheth's new address. And herein lays the key to living a fruitful life and lesson number three. He *moved* to Jerusalem. He applied and appropriated the word of the king. To *appropriate* means "to take to one's self, to claim or use." It wouldn't have profited Mephibosheth if he had stayed in Lo Debar and didn't claim his inheritance. All that was offered to him was in Jerusalem: the best land and, most of all, the king's table! He had to move. He had to take his place at the king's table. We too have been given a place to come dine with our King. But we need to *move* toward the King's table. He's given us precious promises to live by, but if we neglect to take them in our hearts and apply them to our lives then we are missing out on all God has for us.

Since my mother-in-law passed away, my sister-in-law has had the responsibility of dealing with an empty house and all the stuff that was left behind. With her two brothers living out of the country, she is the only one able to do all this. Legally my sister-in-law has the right by ownership to claim and take whatever she wants in the house. It's all based on her relationship with the one who holds the title deed to the house. She actually felt bad about taking towels, dishes and other things. But it's all hers, right?

The Lord has given us a treasury of goods so to speak. He's given us His love, joy, peace, patience, kindness, goodness, faithfulness and self-control, as well as strength for the weary, comfort for the broken-hearted, hope for the hopeless and promises that we can stand on. It's all there for the taking. Should we miss out on all our King has made available to us because we neglect to take what is ours by faith? He has limitless blessings and victories for us, but if we don't appropriate them we are the ones who miss out. Where would you rather live? In Lo Debar, a barren wilderness, or in Jerusalem dining at the king's table?

Lesson number four: Mephibosheth took a step of faith in coming to the King. He found the kindness of the king and so much more. Take your King's hand that is held out to you in such love. Take for yourself the grace, the power of His promises, the peace that passes understanding, and own them for yourself. Take them to your heart and mind and make them your own possession. My husband and I had just bought his mom a beautiful Herend pottery vase for her 70th birthday last June. It's just sitting in an empty house not being used or enjoyed by anyone. I wanted my sister-in-law to have it, so I asked her to pick it up and take it home with her. We need to do the same. Embrace all that your King has for you. The enemy would lie and try to keep us living in poverty, being barren and unproductive. He doesn't want to see us living a fruitful, victorious life. His plan is to keep us fearful, fretting the future and focused on self.

My friend Terry used to say, "Possess your possessions." Seize the Word of God daily. Own it for yourself. No one else can do this for you. Synonyms for *appropriate* are embrace, hold, enjoy, belong to, in possession of, ownership and allotment. Joshua 13-17 talks about the allotment for the tribes of Israel. God had brought them to a land flowing with milk a honey, a fruitful land indeed. Even after coming into the Promised Land, there was still much land to possess. In reality they only possessed a small percentage of what God had intended for them to have. They still had to go out in battle and take what God had given them. It was theirs on paper but practically they had to make it their own.

Thankfully our enemy is a defeated foe, but he's not going away quietly. Each day we have a choice to make. Will we go to the Word of God and claim more territory? Will we take our place at the King's table? It's there we see our faithful King and find His very character a source of hope and encouragement. As you do just that, the Lord will make your life fruitful and use you to accomplish His eternal purposes. Like Mephibosheth you will find yourself dining with the king, eternally blessed and a recipient of the king's kindness. Enjoy your King and hold on tight to His Word!

The ABCs of God's Goodness

But the fruit of the Spirit
is love . . . goodness (benevolence).
Galatians 5:22

Chapter 43

The Lord has been so good to us. His heart is to *do* good for His children. The goodness of God is revealed in His actions toward us. Kindness expresses His heart of love and grace.

When my twelve-year-old son went to junior high winter camp, his dad put some extra money in his wallet. As a loving father, he wanted to make sure his son had enough money for the camp picture as well as a few snacks for the duration of the trip. What motivated my husband was a heart filled with loving kindness, the act itself was his goodness being demonstrated. Jesus "went about doing good" (Acts 10:38). David penned Psalm 119:68, "You are good and do good." As we go through the ABCs we will see just a few of the many blessings that have been extended to us because of God's goodness. There is no denying the action which is backed up by His kindness.

A—We have *access* to the very presence of God.
B—He has placed us in the *body* of Christ.

C—He *comforts* us by His Word, through the Holy
    Spirit.

D—He's *delivered* us from the enemy, sin and our
    flesh.

E—We will spend *eternity* with Him!

F—We've been *forgiven* our sins, we have a
    heavenly Father who loves us!

G—God's *grace* has been lavished upon us:
    unmerited, unearned, undeserved!

H—He's given us His *Holy Spirit* and He is our
    living *hope*.

I—We have an *inheritance* that is incorruptible and
    will not fade away.

J—*Jesus*. Who else? For He has come to take away
    our sins.

K—The *kindness* of the King.

L—The limitless *love* of God, always
    unconditional.

M—His matchless *mercy*, overlooking our offenses,
    not treating us as we deserve.

N—We are *never* alone. We have His promise.
    Nothing can separate us from Him.

O—He is *omnipotent*, possessing unlimited power
    which is available to us.

P—We have His *peace*, His *promises*, His *presence*
    with us and *prayer*.

Q—He is the ultimate thirst *quencher*, quenching
    our soul.

R—We've been *ransomed*, *redeemed*, *rescued* and
    released from captivity.

S—We've been *saved*, set free from Satan's grip
    and hold.

T—There is a *treasury* of gifts and blessings opened to us which are just priceless.

U—We are *united* with God and other believers through Jesus Christ.

V—We have been given *victory* through the cross of Christ.

W—We have His *Word* which is a lamp to our feet and a light to our path.

X—We have the *excellence* of His kingdom to look forward to.

Y—*YHWH*, Jehovah, the permanent being. He's fixed, unchanging and eternal.

Z—We have a new *zip code.* As believers, our citizenship is in heaven. This world is not our home; we are just passing through! How good is that?

I encourage you to make your own list of God's goodness. It is a wonderful reminder of all He has done for us. Celebrate His goodness and give thanks to the Lord for He is good! May we grow to be like our Father, extending His goodness to those around us.

"But You are God, ready to pardon, gracious and merciful, slow to anger, abundant in kindness, and did not forsake them [the Children of Israel—and us for that matter]. . . . You also gave Your good Spirit to instruct them, and did not withhold Your manna from their mouth, and gave them water for their thirst" (Neh. 9:17,20).

The Lord is Faithful

So do not fear, for I am with you;
do not be dismayed, for I am your God.
I will strengthen you and help you; I will uphold
you with My righteous right hand.
Isaiah 41:10

Chapter 44

Faithfulness. It's an attribute that describes our God perfectly. *Faithful* is "firm in adherence to the truth." Jesus is the Way, the *Truth* and the Life. Faithful means "constant in the performance of duties or services." Jesus faithfully fulfilled His mission in redeeming mankind, performing the greatest display of love when He chose to die on the cross for us. He came to do that which we could never attempt or even think to do. Faithful is "exact, in conformity to the letter and spirit." He satisfied the requirements of the Law, living a perfect, sinless life. In Hebrews 1:3, speaking of Jesus it says, "The Son is the radiance of God's glory and the *exact* representation of His being, sustaining all things by His powerful word." Jesus is constant, not fickle, without failure, without defect, fraud, trick or ambiguity. When Philip said to Jesus, "Show us the Father," Jesus replied, "Have I been with you so long, and yet you have not known Me, Philip? He who has seen Me has seen the Father"

(John 14:9). Jesus is in every way the exact *likeness* of His Father. He is with *precise accuracy* a representation of God's love, grace, kindness and faithfulness. Synonyms for *faithfulness* are singleness of heart, man of honor, man of his word, truthful! Jesus had a *single* purpose when He took on human flesh as God incarnate. It wasn't to make a better you, but to make a new you! He is the best example of a Man who keeps His word, as we will see. Five truths to take note of:

First, who is making the promise? GOD ALMIGHTY, the Lord God Omnipotent! Nothing is too hard for Him. He flung the universe in order by a single sentence. He who called you is faithful, who also will do it. We must always consider the source of the promise or word. The Lord is a Man of His word. He will not go back on His word.

Secondly, what does He promise? To finish what He started. Jesus is 100% committed to finishing what He begins. Some think Jesus could have been a finish carpenter, designing furniture. He wouldn't start a project and leave it incomplete. I loved the scene from the *Passion* where Jesus has his mother sit in a chair at the raised table He designed. It was something contrary to the custom of the day, where people sat on the floor. She thought it would never catch on. But Jesus knew better. She sat with confidence in the chair He constructed. It was a finished work and that of beauty. There is no doubt that whatever the Lord sets out to do in us, He will finish it. I have numerous little projects throughout my home that I've started over the years—some complete, some are still a work in progress. There are cabinets that still need painting, photo albums that still need to be finished, and hopefully someday I'll get to them but there's no guarantee. Jesus isn't a *someday* God. He's faithful and He has a plan. He's on top of it, whatever *it* is in your life. He will see you through to the finish line. He saved us. He rescued us all by His amazing grace and He will see us safely to heaven.

The third truth to note is that the Lord only does *good* work. He alone is good and does good. His work is never shabby or insufficient. He's a master craftsman. What He is doing in our lives presently is a good work. *Good* means strong, abundant, fit and complete. God's plan is to make us fit for heaven. He is making us stronger each day as He enlarges our hearts with more of His love, more patience and more joy. We exercise our bodies to be healthy, to be fit and to firm up our muscles. In order for that to happen, we must workout. The Lord has a workout plan for us in the realm of faith. The trials we go through are in a sense like spiritual exercise. It takes faith in Jesus to go through a trial, knowing we will come out the other side. It takes trust in who God says He is, that He's got it all under control. It takes a certain belief that He hears me when I cry out to Him. And a belief that He will answer me when I call. We are His *workmanship* (Eph. 2:10)! He is at work in each of us and it's a good thing.

Fourth, when God says, "I will," it's a guarantee. We live in a day where there are not many absolutes. But this is one thing we can rest assured on. Has He ever gone back on His word? Of course not. Has there ever been a saint in all of history that didn't get an answer to their prayers? We may get a *no* or a *wait*, maybe even *not my timing*, but we'll always get an answer. As a mother, I have never purposely ignored my kids. (Well, maybe once or twice when I was really sick or recovering from a surgery and I knew their Dad was home to take care of them.) The Lord doesn't have sick days; He never goes on vacation or needs a day off. His ear is continually open to His kids. He answers every prayer immediately. It may be some time before we see the fruition of His answer, but we can be confident He has heard our plea. "At the beginning of your supplications the command went out" (Daniel 9:23).

When God says, "I will," He means business. In Ezekiel Chapter 36, the Lord is speaking about the restoration of Israel to the land. Twenty-one times the Lord says, "I will," as He established a new covenant with Israel. Here are just a few of them: "I will give you a new heart . . . I will remove the heart of stone. . . . I will put My Spirit within you. . . . I will be your God. . . . I will save you. . . . I, the Lord, have spoken and will do it!" And He did. He kept His word to the Children of Israel. In 1948, Israel became a nation. God gave them the land and re-gathered His people as a nation.

We can trust our greatest cares and concerns to Him. He will see us through. He will answer when we call out to Him. He will make a way. He promises in Isaiah 46:4, "I will be the same . . . I will bear you. . . . I will carry you . . . I will deliver you." "My purpose will be established, and I will accomplish all My good pleasure. . . . I will bring it to pass. . . . I have planned it, surely I will do it" (Isa. 46:10-11). "Do not call to mind the former things, or ponder things of the past. Behold, I will do something new, now it will spring forth. . . . I will even make a roadway in the wilderness" (Isa. 43:18-19). "I will lead the blind by a way they do not know . . . I will guide them. I will make darkness into light before them" (Isa. 42:16).

When the Great I Am says, "I will," stand still and watch Him work. (It's better than the latest 3D movie!) We have an awesome God who is able to work wonders on our behalf. Oh, beloved sister in Christ, hear His heart for you today. He will come through for you; He loves you so very much. He would say to you, "I will strengthen you, surely I will help you, surely I will uphold you with My righteous right hand." (Isa. 41:10). He has promised, "I will never desert you" (Heb. 13:5). The Amplified Bible says it this way, "I will not in any way fail you nor give you up nor leave you without support. [I will] not, [I will] not, [I will] not in any degree leave you helpless nor forsake nor let [you] down (relax My hold on you)! [Assuredly not!]"

I sure hope all those *I wills* bring you comfort and confidence in your God so that you too may say, "The Lord is my Helper; I will not be seized with alarm [I will not fear or dread or be terrified]. What can man do to me?" (Heb. 13:6). His Word does bring us hope. May each of God's *I wills* bring you to a place of greater faith in Him, greater trust in who He says He is and a greater belief that our God is able to do exceedingly abundantly above all that we ask or think.

The fruit of the Spirit is love, evidenced by God's faithfulness through the life of Christ. As we abide in Him, Lord willing, others will catch a glimpse of His faithfulness in our lives as well. And then we will be those living testimonies of God's faithfulness. Just the other day my husband and I discovered we had a slab leak under our kitchen. There was a hot spot in front of the dishwasher and we could hear the sound of running water. Sure enough, the plumber confirmed our suspicion. He successfully re-routed the pipes and took care of the leak. Since it was a slab leak, our association covered 100% of the bill. The Lord is so faithful. Share your story of God's faithfulness with someone today and praise His holy name.

"Therefore know that the Lord your God, He is God, the faithful God who keeps covenant and mercy for a thousand generations with those who love Him and keep His commandments" (Deut. 7:9).

As I Was with Moses

As I was with Moses, so I will be with you:
I will not fail you, nor forsake you.
Joshua 1:5

Chapter 45

Moses had quite the task of leading the Children of Israel out of Egypt. There were possibly two million people in that multitude of an exodus. Parents and children, grandparents, aunts, uncles and cousins, not to mention friends—and you thought your family camping trip was a challenge. For nearly forty years, God faithfully provided for ALL those people in the wilderness. He graciously sent them manna in the morning every single day. Do you know how many days of provision that covered? 40 years x 365 days = 14,600 days! Now each of those two million people probably ate three times a day—that's 2,000,000 x 3 = 6,000,000 meals per day (manna muffins, manna bread, manna on toast, over easy, sunny side up, however they prepared it—after a few months I'm sure they got creative). So figure 6,000,000 meals per day x 14,600 days and that's 87,600,000,000 meals. I can't even comprehend the magnitude of manna God faithfully sent each morning so that they would have enough to carry them through the day. Is God faithful or what? This is off the charts; literally, my little calculator doesn't have enough space for all those zeros.

What a beautiful picture of our faithful God providing for the needs of His precious Children. Were they really all that precious? Didn't they murmur and complain and even wish to go back to Egypt? Yes, they did. But God in His love and faithfulness considered them precious in His sight as He does us. The Lord has manna for us too. Each day His Word is available to us with manifold blessings abounding with goodness for our souls. His Word is there as a lamp to our feet and a light to our path. He's provided the nourishment we need to live each day. The Children of Israel were to gather manna one day at a time and then only once a week were they given a double portion to carry them through on the Sabbath. Dear sister, come to the plentiful table that He has so richly prepared. If He could sustain two million plus people for forty years in the wilderness, surely He is able to sustain and maintain our lot as well. How do we become fruitful in a barren wilderness? We tap into God's provision, His Holy Spirit, and partake every day from his supply of love and kindness. We take His promises as our very own.

As the baton was being handed over to Joshua from Moses, I'm sure this promise brought him great encouragement and comfort: "As I was with Moses, so I will be with you: I will not fail you, nor forsake you" (Josh. 1:5). If I were Joshua, the thought going through my mind would be, "Okay, God was good and faithful for Moses in all that He did for Him, but can He do that for me?" Why do we doubt God's goodness? It seems as though it's always easier to have faith in God for others and their circumstances. Sure, God can rescue or deliver them. But do we believe that He can and will do the same for us? Maybe it's our own insecurities or fears that keep us from believing. Or perhaps it's the whispers of the enemy that sow those seeds of doubt. Joshua needed God's assurance for all the battles he would face. Is there any greater source of confidence that bolsters our faith than the very promise of God that He is with us? The same faithfulness that was displayed for Moses would be extended to Joshua. As Joshua looked back in His mind over all those years and remembered the vast resources Jehovah Jireh had sent forth—shoes that didn't wear out, manna day after day after day and water from the rock—He must have marveled at God's goodness. It gave him the strength to face the day.

If God can see 2,000,000 people through the wilderness and provide 87,600,000,000 meals over a forty year span, surely He will be faithful to you and me. He didn't fail Moses. He didn't fail Joshua either. Joshua's parting words testify to God's faithfulness: "Behold, this day I am going the way of all the earth. And you know in all your hearts and in all your souls that not one thing has failed of all the good things which the Lord your God spoke concerning you. All have come to pass for you; not one word of them has failed" (Josh. 23:14). Wow, what a powerful testimony. Can we all say, "AMEN, Joshua!"? The Lord did deliver his people from the oppression of Pharaoh. He walked with them in the wilderness guiding them with the pillar of fire by night and the cloud by day; giving them shade and rest from the scorching desert sun and warmth on those cold desert nights. He crossed them over the Jordan into the Promised Land and gave them victory from their enemies. In every aspect of their lives God proved himself faithful—spiritually, physically, emotionally. He was there.

Where do we look for assurance and confidence? The cross! Jesus will cross us over to victory because He won the war at the cross. Yes, there are still battles and places we need to trust the Lord in on a daily basis. But Jesus would say to you and me today, "As I was with Moses, so shall I be with you. My supply has not run dry. My faithfulness is still available to you." Whatever your need may be, He is able to do exceedingly abundantly above all we could ever ask or think. Our greatest need was being reconciled to God. Jesus cried, "It is finished," declaring the work of salvation complete—a done deal! Our debt has been paid in full, the account is fully settled. May you rest in God's faithful provision. And may you testify as Joshua did that not one of God's promises have ever failed you either.

"He spread a cloud for a covering, and fire to give light in the night. The people asked, and He brought quail, and satisfied them with the bread of heaven. He opened the rock, and water gushed out" (Ps. 105:39-41).

Genuine Gentleness

Learn from Me, for I am gentle and lowly in heart.
Matthew 11:29

Chapter 46

Sometimes it's easier to know what something is by knowing what it isn't. We are told in Galatians 5 what the works of the flesh are. Let me prepare you; it is not a pretty picture. Are you sitting down? Okay, just a few characteristics of our flesh are "hatred, contentions . . . outbursts of wrath, selfish ambitions." But it gets worse when we compare ourselves in the light of who God is. Then it's downright ugly. We need to see ourselves in the light of what God's Word says. Comparing ourselves to others will not give us the accurate truth. It's the Word of God that speaks the truth in love to our hearts, not to scare us off or to condemn us, but to woo us unto Himself that He might fill us with more of Himself. The fruit of the Spirit is love which is manifested through: the joy we have in the Holy Spirit, the peace He sends us in the midst of calamity, the patience He imparts to us in the trials we endure, the kindness of our King unto us, His faithfulness to His character and promises, and now we come to His gentleness.

Gentleness isn't rage, madness, fuming, losing one's temper, exploding, boiling over, ranting and raving.

Our sin nature left to itself is uncontrollable, ungovernable and hot-tempered. I told you it wasn't going to be pretty. Have you ever behaved in a manner found in that list? I have. In our flesh we are prone to fly off the handle, fume over things and occasionally explode on any given day at any given moment. But our gracious, loving Lord won't leave us there. He is in the business of transformation! And I say, "Hallelujah, thank you, Jesus!" Who of us wants to behave like that on a daily basis? It's awful and it's sin. It's unbecoming behavior for the Christian woman. The more of Him that fills my life, the less of my flesh there is to contend with. The Lord works from the inside out in our lives. It begins with His Spirit living within our hearts as we bring ourselves under the authority of the Holy Spirit. His power then begins that inner work of transformation. Imagine your life having a construction sign out in front: Work in Progress. The key for us is submission. (I accidently misspelled submission when typing and it came out *sunmission*. That's what we need to do, submit to the SON!) I know when the word submission is spoken, many women cringe. It's not a problem when you know WHO you are submitting to. Full and glad surrender is a joy when it's unto the One who is the Savior of your soul. Coming to the cross in communion is where we remember Him and all He did for us. How can we not gladly bow our knee to Him? Give Him the access necessary to mold you and make you more like Jesus. That's the Father's goal for our lives and it ought to be ours too.

Jesus is the genuine gentleman. He's not rough or

harsh. His words were and are so soothing, so comforting. His temper, His voice, His nature was peaceable, tame, mild and meek. The word *meek* has the idea behind it of flowing liquid. When liquid is poured out does it resist? No, it just flows. Depending on the source of liquid it can be quite powerful. Jesus was just that, so mighty, so full of power, yet so gentle, humble. He was not easily provoked or irritated. He was ever yielding to His Father's will and mission. We too are to be poured out like a drink offering, flowing with His gentleness and love.

Submission surrenders to the Savior's sovereignty. As we come to the Lord on a daily basis we must recognize His supremacy and authority over our lives and take action. How do we do this? We do this through prayer, through a song in our hearts and through bending our knee to Him. Submission may take many forms: obedience to His will over mine, resignation, yielding without murmuring, giving up control to be governed by another. It also means to give up resistance, to give way and lay down one's arms, basically unresisting. We will continue to look at the example of our Lord and His gentleness for further instruction in the next chapter. Ask the Lord to begin that transformation in your heart of His gentle nature and gentle spirit. Surrender your heart to Him in those moments when you sense your flesh flaring up. Submit to your Savior; it's the way to victorious, fruitful living.

The Gentleness of Christ

Father, if You are willing,
remove this cup from Me; yet not
My will, but Yours be done.
Luke 22:42

Chapter 47

Where do we see the gentleness of our Savior? In His suffering. There's no better place than in the garden of Gethsemane and at the cross to learn from our Savior's example. He came on bended knees fully accepting His call to die. With all the power that He could have accessed to escape the cross, He chose rather to acquiesce to His Father's will. In quiet resignation He bled great drops of blood. In the face of mocking crowds and hurling insults He uttered not a rebuke. In love and gentleness He said, "Father, forgive them; for they know not what they do" (Luke 23:34). Has the world ever seen such gentleness? Perfect obedience. Absolute surrender. Total abandonment. The gentleness that Jesus displayed required humility which humbled itself to the point of death, the death of the cross.

It was in the garden when the soldiers came to take Jesus away that Peter struck the High Priest's servant's ear off. Jesus in perfect calmness told Peter to put away his sword. It was not the time to fight, but the time to forge ahead in full surrender. Gentleness lays down one's arms. It simply gives up the fight. When we are prone to fight in our flesh, gentleness gives way; it's unresisting and compliant. Jesus said, speaking of His life, "No one takes it away from Me. On the contrary, I lay it down voluntarily" (John 10:18). When it came time for Jesus to be crucified, He didn't resist the cross or the nails that would soon pierce His hands. With quiet presence of mind, He laid down his arms, offering them upon that wooden beam awaiting his fate. It was the entire purpose of why He came. Gentleness gives up the fight and is willing to face death's final blow. What about us?

Are we willing to die to our flesh? Will you die to your own agenda? Don't be afraid to surrender. Look to Jesus, the one you are yielding to. Your suffering Savior is now the risen Christ. The lesson for us is that in dying we live. When we lose our life we find it. When we are obedient to the Lord and humble ourselves before Him, He lifts us up (1 Peter 5:6). "God resists the proud, but gives grace to the humble" (James 4:6). There is victory through His death for us. We have a living hope as the result (1 Peter 1:3).

I encourage you, precious sister in Christ, in the quietness of your heart ask the Lord to teach you and train you in humility. Bow down before Him on your knees and surrender all that is on your heart. As you do, He will exchange your nature for His. He will take your temper and give you His gentleness. Submit yourself to His Lordship and allow Him to take over.

Stop fighting, stop resisting, and yield to Him. Surrender and submission are at the heart of God's gentleness. And they will open the door to a fruitful, productive life that brings Him glory.

G—God came down to redeem mankind.

E—Emanuel, entirely submitting to His Father's will.

N—"Not My will, but Yours be done."

T—Teaching us by example to die with calm composure.

L—Laying down His life in full surrender.

E—Emptying Himself, He yielded in humility.

N—Never looking to save His life, He willingly laid it down.

E—Every power to escape, yet He chose to die.

S—Suffering Savior.

S—Submission to the King!

The Heart of Gentleness

He must increase, but I must decrease. [He must grow more prominent; I must grow less so.]
John 3:30

Chapter 48

At the heart of gentleness is a life marked by two qualities: surrender and humility. First, gentleness requires complete surrender, which is wholly submitted to God and His will. Second, gentleness brings humility which is revealed in a life that is willing to bow down before God, being fully dependent on Him and Him alone. In order for that to happen, we need to be free from self and its pull on our spirit. The flesh wars against the spirit. Our sin nature is truly wretched, as we have seen. The works of the flesh that display fits of rage and outbursts of wrath are the very things that the Lord desires to transform. He has a new nature for us, for we are new creations in Christ once we come to Him. Imagine you are returning a garment which is the wrong size to the store. The employee gladly exchanges it for one that fits properly. Well, as a new creature in Christ, those behaviors of the flesh don't fit us as women who long to live fruitful lives. Losing our tempers, exploding in anger, having our impatience boiling over, ranting and raving to our kids ought not be. We need to put on the Lord Jesus and make no provision for the flesh (Rom. 13:14).

How do I have victory over my flesh and gain His heart of gentleness? Completely surrender and humble yourself before God. True humility knows the truth about who we are and who we aren't. We are sinful. We've missed the mark. If there is any doubt to your sinfulness, just read the list in Galatians 5:19-21 and ask the Lord to give you a glimpse of your heart. Be prepared, it might shock you. But the good news is that the Lord already knows. And He loves you in spite of yourself. As we see ourselves for who we truly are, it causes us to praise God all the more for His amazing grace "that saved a wretch like me."

John Newton penned those words in "Amazing Grace." He knew his own wretchedness, sinful condition and unworthiness. There's no dressing up sin and trying to make it look good. Our sinful nature is vile, guilty and abominable before a Holy God. There is no good thing within us. Acknowledging our sin to God opens the door for Him to bring reconciliation, restoration and transformation.

Humility comes on bended knees to God for pardon and redemption. It comes with true remorse and regret over the sin that nailed Jesus to the cross. It repents over behaviors and attitudes and agrees with God's assessment of who we are. The humble heart has felt the hand of God reach out with love, acceptance and forgiveness. It's when our hearts have been melted by God's grace that we are awed at His acceptance of us. Then and only then is a humble heart born and gentleness enters in.

Who was the greatest man in Scripture, apart from our Lord? John the Baptist. Jesus said there was no one greater (Matt. 11:11). John sought to put Jesus in the place of prominence when he said, "He must become greater; I must become less" (John 3:30). What made John so great in the eyes of Jesus? His humility. When people see our lives, it ought to be Jesus and His influence that they notice. The moment of greatness in our life comes when we decrease and He increases. Let the gentleness of God be seen through you. John moved out of the way so that it was the Lamb, first and foremost—His splendor and majesty, glory and grandeur—that shined forth. John knew his place was to be a voice for the Lord. He was dedicated and devoted to living a life that diminished, while the Lord was magnified. Gentleness is emptied of selfish ambitions and is all about the Lamb who takes away the sins of the world. John's life was absorbed in His Savior.

How do we have a heart like John's? We magnify the Lord and esteem others. What's one way you can show Jesus you regard Him? Praise Him! Extol Him! Lavish Him with your love and adoration. Philippians 2:3 says, "Do nothing out of selfish ambition or vain conceit, but in humility consider others better than yourselves." How do we practically esteem others? Esteem means to respect, regard and show consideration of. Here are several suggestions:

- Value others, listen more to what they have to say. Our flesh wants to talk about its favorite subject: self. Don't let it rule the conversation.

- Resign to talking less, and don't interrupt when someone else is speaking.
- Ask questions about the other person and their interests, keeping the conversation on them. This shows you regard them and place higher value on their life than yours. Remember a gentle heart is willing to give way and yield.
- Seek out wise counsel from one or two godly friends and realize they know more than you do. Have a teachable heart.
- Take a risk and humble your heart; making yourself vulnerable with a friend shows a gentle spirit. You don't have to know everything or have it all together. And it's okay to cry as you share your heart.
- Pray for others, not just your immediate family or needs.
- Love people enough by exercising patience, kindness and respect.
- Give preference through deference. Defer to others. Make a conscious decision before you get out of bed in the morning and leave the house. Choose to have this mindset: "Let each regard the others as better than and superior to himself [thinking more highly of one another than you do of yourselves]" (Phil. 2:3).
- Prefer others. Purpose in your heart to put them first. Gentleness shows restraint, control and command of oneself. How we need to live under the command and authority of the Holy Spirit!

I just have to share this last story as it fits perfectly with preferring others and seeing a gentle heart in action. I recently asked my twelve-year-old son to help empty the dishwasher. He was so quick to cooperate. There was no fight, no battle, just total compliance to my request. It honestly caused me to marvel at his gentleness that chose to prefer his mom's will. Now enter my fourteen-year-old son who was asked to load the dishes: "You want me to load the dishes?" "Yes I do," I replied. "Okay, I'll do it." No resistance, just obedience. One gentle heart is a beautiful thing. And two gentle hearts are even better. The best thing of all is I didn't lose my temper once because they were so quick to yield. That's three hearts on their way to gentleness. To God be the glory, great things He has done!

"Therefore, as God's chosen people, holy and dearly loved, clothe yourselves with compassion, kindness, humility, gentleness and patience" (Col. 3:12).

Enough Is Enough

Everything is permissible (allowable and lawful) for me; but not all things are helpful (good for me to do, expedient and profitable when considered with other things). Everything is lawful for me, but I will not become the slave of anything or be brought under its power.
1 Cor. 6:12

Chapter 49

"All things are lawful for me, but I will not be mastered by anything." What is mastering you? Who is your master? Is it Jesus or your flesh? Self-control is the final manifestation of the fruit of the Spirit in Galatians 5:23. The questions before us are important ones. Who rules over your life? Is the Holy Spirit ruling and reigning, or is your flesh untamed and unrestrained? There was a time in my life, years ago, when I struggled with an eating disorder. I was nineteen years old then, and by God's grace and goodness He gave me victory from that bondage. It's been many years since that time and, thinking back upon it, I certainly was in bondage to my flesh. It dictated my behavior for the day. That ought not to be so for the mature believer. I am so grateful to the Lord for His deliverance and help as He taught me not to be a slave to food. The Lord showed me the importance of allowing Him to take control of my choices—even down to the food I eat.

I believe it was A.W. Tozer who looked himself in the mirror in the morning and gave his flesh a warning, "You're only getting 3 meals today." He was putting his flesh on notice. That's what we need to do. Self-control is all about being under God's control. Tell your flesh nature, "Enough is enough!" I've heard someone say, "Be ruthless with yourself and merciful with others." We live in a day where self-indulgence is out of control. We don't know how to simply say "NO!" to our flesh. I do try to practice saying *no* to my flesh once a day at the very least— whether it's with the food I wish I could eat or sleeping in or just sitting down to watch the news. The Lord has had to teach me to be stricter with my eating habits. And I have *learned* that sometimes it is wise to say "just one or two bites" or "not now" or just "no." Believe me, this didn't come overnight. For years food has been an issue for me, but it's been something I have had to learn. I am still a work in progress and still learning. If I had the liberty to eat brownies every day, I would gladly jump at the chance. But that is not going to help me walk in love and in self-control; I'd be a slave to my flesh if I allowed that to happen. Paul said, "I have learned in whatever state I am, to be content" (Phil. 4:12). I am still learning daily how to bring my life under the lordship of Jesus. It really boils down to the fact that I need to love God more than I love my flesh.

Every day brings new opportunities to die to our

flesh! One specific way to train your flesh is to place limits and boundaries on it. Just like when my kids were toddlers, I had the baby gate up to keep them in their room for their quiet play time so I could take a shower. They were confined. No way out. That little gate kept them safe and secure. We need parameters and boundaries for our flesh to keep us safe. Even now with my ten-year-old daughter, I am beginning to teach her how to discipline her flesh and to say no when it comes to sweets. Our flesh will forever crave this or that and want more, more and more. It will never be satisfied or content on its own. Unless it has been overfed on Thanksgiving or Christmas—and then you probably wish you had said *no* or *no more* to begin with. It's when the Holy Spirit fills us with more of Himself that we find true contentment. It's Jesus and His presence that our souls truly crave. Once we fill the void with God, then we are finally satisfied. The key is do not let your tank run on empty. Be filled with the Spirit continuously.

The enemy is continually seeking to make us a slave, either to Him or to our flesh. True freedom lies in Jesus being Lord and master of our life (John 8:36). When Jesus is Lord and ruling over our life, our flesh is then brought in submission to Him. Our flesh is actually to be reckoned dead, mortified, yes, crucified with Christ (Gal. 2:20). Give notice to your flesh today, "Enough is enough!" "Reckon yourselves to be dead indeed to sin, but alive to God" (Rom. 6:11).

Purpose with a Passion

But Daniel purposed in his heart that he would
not defile himself with the portion of the king's
delicacies, nor with the wine which he drank.
Daniel 1:8

Chapter 50

What happens when we lack purpose to our lives? We end up living with our flesh in control instead of living with self-control—or as other versions word it, temperance, continence and self-restraint (Gal. 5:23). Two men in the Bible were both called of God, Daniel and Samson. As we look at both their lives, one chose to follow the Lord and deny his flesh, the other gave into his flesh and lived a life without restraint.

There are lessons to be learned from Daniel's life. First, he purposed in his heart that he would not defile himself. What does it mean to live with purpose? It means to live with resolve, determination and will. Daniel lived with strength of mind that when he was faced with a choice to make he already knew in his heart what he should do. He must have learned from an early age to exercise self-restraint and to take a stand. The influence of godly parents in his life no doubt shaped his future. Those convictions didn't just happen haphazardly or on his own. It takes a resolute heart and mind to train up a child in the way they should go. Even though Daniel is probably a young teenager he shows incredible backbone, an unflinching mind and unyielding spirit that was able to say no to the influence of the king's delicacies. The pressure and pull of a pagan king did not sway his heart to compromise. What a wonderful example he is to us.

Not only did Daniel have a purposed heart but he clearly had a plan which he thought about ahead of time. When faced with temptation he was able to stand firm and stand strong in his convictions. It's much easier to face a temptation with a plan. Every Sunday morning there are free doughnuts after church, and every Sunday I go in with a plan to not give in and eat what I know would be oh so yummy. I would imagine, long before the road to Babylon, Daniel's parents had taught him what was right and wrong. So when he was with his friends he was able to go into captivity with a plan. If we are asked to do something that would cause us to compromise, we must with God's help take a stand. They say the best offense is a good defense. The Lord was surely Daniel's defense!

"Now God had brought Daniel into the favor and goodwill of the chief of the eunuchs" (Dan. 1:9). The Lord had certainly given Daniel favor as well as a heart that was determined to put God first. He deliberately chose *on purpose* to stay pure: "But Daniel made up his mind that he would not defile himself" (Dan. 1:8). Daniel had a choice to make: to compromise his beliefs or carry out what he knew to be God's will for his life. We so need the influence of God's Spirit to help us walk in a way that is right in His sight. Knowing where we are heading determines how we are going to behave. An interesting synonym for *purpose* is object. It speaks of a destination, a goal, a target. Daniel's goal was to not defile himself. His aim was to please the Lord and put Him first. What is your goal and aim as you live in this corrupt world? Is your goal heaven, and your heart's desire is to please God rather than your own flesh? The byproduct of living a fruitful life is self-control. If we are to live as Daniel did than our hearts must be fixed and purposed to live in such a way that we don't drift away from our target. This is where Samson fell as will see in the next chapter.

We usually associate the word *premeditate* in a negative way. It speaks of forethought and planning ahead; most often in the context of a crime that establishes a clear intent to carry out an objective, like robbing a bank or even worse murder. But let's look at it in a positive light. If we break down the word it simply means to think beforehand. What if we thought ahead with a plan to walk in purity and not do anything that would cause us to compromise our faith? It might be the simple rule that we don't watch R-rated movies or even PG-13 movies these days. Or it could be a boundary that says no alcohol, period! What would our day look like if we said to ourselves we are not going to indulge our flesh or give in to its cravings? What if we determined with God's help to say, "I am *bent on intentionally deciding* to say *no* to my flesh and more importantly *yes* to God. Yes, I

222

want the Lord to take command of my life. I don't want anything in this world to have power over me."

Lastly the passion of Daniel's parents became his own. Daniel's first passion was the Lord. His desire was for God. He devoted himself to God. As parents we have the responsibility of passing on the Word to our kids to train them up in the Lord, but at some point they must embrace the Lord on their own. They must take ownership of their relationship with God. I want to live my life like Daniel did: passionately living for my Lord, pursuing Him with my whole heart, pleasing Him every step of the way. I want to have purpose to my life and the choices I make I want to clearly aid in arriving to my ultimate destination which is heaven. I also pray my kids grow in their relationship with the Lord and have a passion to know Him and serve Him. I can't live their walk for them. Daniel had a heart for the Lord that was loyal. Instead of craving the king's delicacies he craved to please his King. Instead of being allured to the carnal pleasures before him he preferred to do it God's way. Instead of giving in to the temptation, he was inclined to deny his flesh; that's what self-control looks like in the life of a fruitful believer.

We see in Daniel's life devotion, dedication and determination. May we live our lives *on purpose* for the Lord. May our decisions and choices be made with the intention of loving God with all our heart, soul, mind and strength. When you love someone you want to please them. Daniel clearly had a heart that loved the Lord and whose aim was to stay pure. His ardent ambition for purity is an example for us all! With God all things are possible (Matt. 19:26). God gave Daniel favor and a fervent heart. He can do the same for us. You just need to ask Him. Bring your flesh in submission to the Lord and have Him take total control. Self-control is really letting God take control. Dare to be a Daniel!

Unless a Grain of Wheat Falls

Truly, truly, I say to you, unless a grain of wheat falls into the earth and dies, it remains alone; but if it dies, it bears much fruit.
John 12:24

Chapter 51

If Daniel's life portrays for us a picture of self-restraint, limits on his flesh and control of his desires, then Samson's life reveals to us the antithesis of self-control. His life is totally out of control, given over to unbridled desire: the lust of his flesh, the lust of his eyes and the pride of life (1 John 2:16).

We read Samson's story in Judges 13-16. It would seem, looking at the choices he made, he never embraced the Lord to be the passion of his life. He disregarded the lifestyle of consecration that was to be his guideline for living: abstain from wine or fermented drink, don't even eat fresh grapes or raisins; don't go near a dead body; and don't let a razor be used on your head (Num. 6:1-7). Parents are to train a child in the way they should go. But when that child grows up, he or she is then responsible for their own choices and actions. Kids at some point must respond personally to God for there to be a relationship. Samson's parents could have very well during his childhood followed the Lord's instructions prescribed in the Nazirite vow. He was their answer to prayer and a gift from the Lord with a calling on his life. No razor had touched his head until that time. But somewhere along the line, Samson grew indifferent to the Lord and lacked a passion for the Lord that we witnessed in Daniel's life. Samson's life is a downward spiral. His indulgence led him to a life with a pattern of sin. If our flesh goes unchecked and unrestrained we are bound to get into trouble.

His first mistake is that he sought after a woman in Philistine country. He saw a Philistine woman and ordered his parents to get her for him as his wife, "For she pleaseth me well" (Judg. 14:1-3). Apparently he forgot that he was supposed to be a man of God, consecrated to the Lord and set apart from pagan women. The pull on our flesh is strong, and we see here the lust of his eyes wins over his ability to say no to his flesh. His parents did try to persuade him in verse 3, "Is there no woman among the daughters of your relatives, or among all our people, that you go to take a wife from the uncircumcised Philistines?" Samson did not learn the lesson of placing restrictions on his life to serve as a safe guard for his spirit. He's totally under the power and control of his carnal desires. It will lead him into further sin. But even when sin abounds, grace abounds. "However, his father and mother did not know that it was of the Lord, for He was seeking an occasion against the Philistines" (Judg. 14:4). I have no explanation for this, but I thank the Lord that even when we don't do what we ought to do the Lord somehow turns it for His purposes. Does this give us an excuse to give in to indulge our flesh? Certainly not! Once we give in to sin and open the door to lust, our flesh is never satisfied and it just craves more.

Sometime later, in the process of pursuing this Philistine woman, Samson kills a lion. Upon finding a swarm of bees in the lion's body, "He scraped the honey into his hands and went on, eating as he went. When he came to his father and mother, he gave some to them and they ate it; but he did not tell them that he had scraped the honey out of the body of the lion" (Judg. 14:9). With this unclean act he defiles himself and his parents. During this time Samson issues a riddle for the men of the city, and his wife is used to deceive him. She eventually is given to a companion of his who had been his friend (Judg. 14:20). Then the unthinkable happens in Judges 16:1, "Samson went to Gaza and saw a harlot there, and went in to her." And just four verses later he falls in love with Delilah. Throughout the rest of the chapter Samson is lulled away in a game with Delilah as she tries to discover the secret of his strength. His strength is gone after Delilah "called for a man and had him shave off the seven locks of his hair" (Judg. 16:19). It is just tragic that Samson started out with such promise but, as verse 20 tells us, "He did not know that the Lord had departed from him."

Samson had so much going for him: gifted with strength from God and a calling on his life. But he chose to indulge in his flesh. He ignored the boundaries God had given to him. The lust of his flesh, the lust of his eyes and the pride of life all led to his downward decline. Blinded by his flesh, thinking he wouldn't suffer the consequences of lust, Samson is finally seized by the Philistines who gouge out his eyes (Judg. 16:21). He's now blinded not only spiritually, but physically too. Samson's story is tragic as he's destroyed by a lifestyle of self-gratification.

May this never happen to any of us because we lack self-control. Samson's life is a warning to us of the demise that sin can bring. Let's learn from his downfall. Don't ignore the Holy Spirit prompting you to say no to your flesh. Samson did call out to the Lord one last time and the Lord did hear him. But his life could have had such influence. And who knows what the Lord could have done through him had he not given in to his flesh. Give your flesh a *restraining order*. We need the Holy Spirit to restrain our fleshly tendencies and desires. Why do 2-year-olds have temper tantrums? Because they hate to be told *no* to what they want. So they arch their back in complete defiance, throw a fit, fall on the ground, kick and scream in a last ditch effort to get their own way. Our flesh hates to be limited. But if we desire to live a fruitful life, victorious in our faith, then we must ask the Lord to develop this final attribute of love in our life. Love God, hate sin. He who seeks to keep his life will lose it, but he who loses his life will find it (Luke 9:24). Paul said, "I die daily" (1 Cor. 15:31).

"Truly, truly, I say to you, unless a grain of wheat falls into the earth and dies, it remains alone; but if it does, it bears much fruit" (John 12:24).

That Your Fruit Would Remain

You did not choose Me, but I chose you and appointed you that you should go and bear fruit, and that your fruit should remain.
John 15:16

Chapter 52

It seems only fitting as we come to our last chapter that we finish with a look at Joseph's life one more time. He is the perfect picture of Jesus, who would lead the way for us into victorious Christian living. After years of trial and hardship, Joseph sees the bigger picture unfold before him as his brothers come for grain in the midst of famine. He says, "For God sent me before you to preserve life" (Gen. 45:5). And again he says, "God sent me before you to preserve for you a remnant in the earth, and to keep you alive by a great deliverance" (Gen. 45:7). I have found this to be true: the greater the need, the greater the grace we find available to us. Great needs open the door for greater grace to flow forth from the Father. The Lord desires to pour out great grace upon our lives, we just need to come and ask. It takes great grace to walk through the trials we face. The key is walking through them and coming out the other side better for it; that's the essence of being fruitful in affliction. Only the Lord can take your great need, whatever it is at this moment, and turn it for good and bring a great deliverance through it.

Who else besides Joseph found themselves in great need? There were many, but we will just touch on two others: Esther and Daniel. Out of their afflictions, the Lord brought forth such fruitfulness, such bounty and such a harvest. He took their sorrows and burdens, and through their weakness and dire situations He was able to work it out all for good. There is nothing too hard for Him. If He did it for them, certainly He is able to do it for us.

Joseph went from a forsaken brother thrown in a pit, to a slave in Egypt, to a falsely accused prisoner and eventually to prime minister, effectively serving the Lord as God delivered him. God was with him each step of the way to preserve a nation and prosper a people. Were there heartaches along the way? Certainly. But was Joseph fruitful in the end? Yes, a fruitful vine whose branches climbed over a wall.

What about Esther's life? She was an orphan who was raised by her older cousin. They lived in Babylon during Israel's captivity. She was taken to the king's harem where she was chosen to be queen. Only then she discovers a death sentence upon her life and her people. She risks death in going before the king to make her request. And once again, out of her great need, she found great grace and favor not only from her husband the king, but also from the King of Kings who was working behind the scenes. Her life was preserved by a faithful God who always works *all* things together for good.

Then there's Daniel, a young teenager who was

taken captive by the Babylonians years before Esther. He's been separated from his family and all that is familiar to him and brought to a pagan country before a pagan king. Daniel never compromises his convictions as a young man or as an adult. That's not to say he lived a perfect life, but we know from Scripture that He purposed in his heart to please the Lord. When facing the decision to pray and stand firm in his faith, he chose to honor God and bow down in submission, humbly praying as He had done for nearly seventy years. When thrown in the lion's den, he too found grace and protection from God. In the face of a hopeless situation, he discovered God is faithful and does deliver! Perhaps Daniel's faith inspired Esther years later.

Each one had their trials and heartaches. And each one found God to be the one who would make them not only fruitful in affliction, but victorious! May God's love so fill us that, no matter what we face, we know that out of it will come a fruitful harvest of joy, peace, patience, goodness, kindness, faithfulness, gentleness and self-control. Seek Him with your whole heart (Matt. 6:33). Ask to be filled with His Spirit every morning as you wake that you might walk victorious in these last days (Ps. 5). May He give you peace to guard your heart and mind that is only found in Him (John 16:33). I pray that He is your reason to rejoice as you find Him to be your rock in a continually shaking world and your refuge from the storms of life (Ps. 71). May He fill you to overflowing that you might endure with patience and perseverance the race set before you (Heb. 12:1). I encourage you to dine daily with the King at His banqueting table, where you will receive the kindness of the King. He longs to lavish His love upon you and do good unto you (1 Sam. 9). God is good and only does good (Ps. 73:1). We may not see it now, but remember those precious saints who pressed on in faith: "Let us not lose heart in doing good, for in due time we will reap if we do not grow weary. So then, while we have opportunity, let us do good to all people, and especially to those who are of the household of the faith" (Gal. 6:9-10). "Faithful is He who calls you, and He also will bring it to pass" (1 Thess. 5:24). If the Lord has you in a dire situation, trust Him that as He was with Moses so shall He be with you and not forsake you (Josh. 1:5). He will bring it to pass. He will not leave you in a place of grief forever. Remember your ABCs of God's character and goodness. He cannot fail! He who was willing to bow in humble submission and surrender to His Father's will is our example in suffering. Accept what the Lord has allowed in your life under the banner of His sovereignty and allow Him to bring healing to your hurting heart. "He sent His word and healed them, and delivered them from their destructions" (Ps. 107:20). The Living Word, the Word that was made flesh and dwelt among us, has given us His Word to encourage and comfort us. And like Daniel, may we all purpose in our hearts to walk in the Spirit and not give in to our flesh. Ask the Lord to restrain your carnal tendencies, lest they take over and bring ruin to your life like Samson's.

Just this morning an 8.9 magnitude earthquake hit

Japan and rocked the Pacific Ocean causing a tsunami warning to be in effect for several countries. We *are* living in the last days. The Lord would have us live fruitful, productive lives for however long we have in this world. With the Lord's strength and grace He can make us a benefit and blessing to our families, friends and community. He desires to use us to advance His eternal purposes and good news (John 3:16). God will use the pain you have gone through, or are going through presently, to be the very tools that bring comfort to another hurting heart. He is the God of ALL COMFORT (2 Cor. 1:3). And the world needs comfort. The world needs the comfort of a God who loves them and died for them and conquered death for them. He gives us comfort so that we will in turn take it and give it out to others (Isa. 61:2). Joseph knew years down the road of suffering that God had meant it all for good. He will take the tragedy of your life and bring something worthwhile to others if you will let him.

The Lord is in the business of turning tragedy into triumph. Just look at the cross. What tragic sorrow Jesus' mother must have endured, as well as the disciples who followed him. What unbearable pain and grief they suffered as they watched Jesus hang on the cross. And yet we call it Good Friday because only God is able to bring beauty from ashes and turn our sorrow into joy (Isa. 61:3 and John 16:20). Resurrection Sunday resonates in our soul as the greatest triumph in all of history! We celebrate Christ's victory over sin, Satan and the grave. One of my new favorite worship songs says, "Christ is risen from the dead! We are one with Him again!" And my other sunrise service favorite to sing is: "Up from the grave He arose, with a mighty triumph o'er His foes, He arose a victor from the dark domain, and He lives forever with His saints to reign. He arose! He arose! Hallelujah, Christ arose!" And there we have our living hope (1 Pet. 1:3)! May you go out with joy and be lead forth with peace living fruitful, triumphant and victorious lives in Christ!

"I give you a new commandment: that you should love one another. Just as I have loved you, so you too should love one another. By this all [men] know that you are My disciples, if you love one another [if you keep on showing love among yourselves]" (John 13:34-35).

"You have not chosen Me, but I have chosen you and I have appointed you [I have planted you], that you might go and bear fruit and keep on bearing, and that your fruit may be lasting [that it may remain, abide]" (John 15:16).

"And now these three remain: faith, hope and love. But the greatest of these is love" (1 Cor. 13:13).

"But the fruit of the Spirit is love, joy, peace, patience, kindness, goodness, faithfulness, gentleness and self-control" (Gal. 5:22-23).

ABOUT THE AUTHOR

Miray Jaksa lives in Lake Forest, CA, with her husband of nearly twenty years and their three children. She gave her life to Christ at ten years old at Calvary Church in Santa Ana, CA. In her late teens she began attending Calvary Chapel Costa Mesa which was her home church for seventeen years. She went on several short term missions trips with the high school ministry and knew the Lord was calling her to the mission field. She stepped out in faith on a longer missions trip to Hungary in 1991, which is where she met her husband. Miray has been homeschooling her kids for ten years now and her favorite subject is history. Calvary Chapel Living Word has been her home church for the past seven years. Writing is a new hobby for her which stems from her love for the Word of God. Her other hobbies include Bible study, homeschooling, reading great books and watching a terrific tennis match (when she has spare time).

Made in the USA
Charleston, SC
09 December 2011